# GIVING VOICE

## A Handbook for Choir Directors & Trainers

David Hill, Hilary Parfitt & Elizabeth Ash

Kevin Mayhew

First published in 1995 by
KEVIN MAYHEW LTD
Rattlesden
Bury St Edmunds
Suffolk IP30 0SZ

ISBN 0 86209 688 X
Catalogue Number 3611172


Book design by Veronica Ward
Artwork and illustrations by Graham Johnstone
Cover: *A Choir of Angels* by the Master of the Lindau Lamentation,
by courtesy of Christie's Images, London


Editor: Alison Sommazzi
Typesetting by Vicky Brown
Music setting by Louise Hill
Printed and bound in Great Britain

# GIVING VOICE

# Contents

# The Authors

DAVID HILL has been Master of Music at Winchester Cathedral since October 1987, and, since 1988, director of the Waynflete Singers. As one of Britain's leading choral conductors, he is in demand at home and abroad as choir trainer, orchestral conductor and organist. Educated at Chetham's School, Manchester, he studied violin, piano and organ. He became a Fellow of the Royal College of Organists at the age of 17. As organ scholar to St John's College, Cambridge, he was assistant to Dr George Guest for four years. He went on to Durham Cathedral as sub-organist, and in 1982 became Master of Music at Westminster Cathedral. From 1980-87 he was musical director of the Alexandria Choir, London, and won the Gramophone award in 1985. He was appointed associate conductor of the Philarmonia Chorus in 1986, and is now its artistic director. David also directs the Royal College of Music Chorus and lectures in Church Music Studies at the Royal Academy of Music, London.

HILARY LLYSTYN PARFITT studied singing, piano and harp at Chetham's School of Music, and later continued her studies at the Guildhall School of Music and Drama with Noelle Barker. In addition to training the chorister awarded the 'Chorister of the Year' in 1992, Hilary has taught the choral scholars and students of the Universities of Durham and Cambridge and in the Junior Department of the Guildhall School of Music. In recent years her work in training boys' voices has involved teaching choristers of Westminster, Winchester, Wells and Bristol Cathedrals and Winchester College. She is increasingly involved in training girls' voices, as a teacher at Rookesbury Park School in Hampshire and with other local groups. She was recently appointed vocal coach to the City of Birmingham Youth Chorus. Hilary is also in demand as a teacher of adults, training voices of both professional and amateurs and coaching choirs. She lectures on voice training at home and abroad.

ELIZABETH ASH is a psychotherapist and education and training consultant. Her work in education over the last twenty five years has increasingly focused on experiential learning and the psychology underlying this. Much of her work has involved developing interactive training materials, including video. She also plans and runs workshops on a variety of topics, particularly on the interplay between the 'personal' and the 'professional'. She is a graduate of the London School of Economics and has spent many years living and working abroad. Singing, as an amateur soloist and in choirs, has always been an important aspect of her life. She continues to have singing lessons.

# Introduction

This book is addressed to all of you who are involved in choir directing and training and who are interested in developing both your own and your choir's skills. It is informed by the experience of the authors, David Hill, Hilary Parfitt and Elizabeth Ash, each of whom, in different but related ways, are concerned with helping others to 'give voice'. We celebrate the serendipity which brought us together and inspired the sharing of our experience and its expression in writing. The idea was triggered by requests to David and Hilary, as they worked in a variety of settings with a range of choral groups, from choir directors concerned about the dearth of useful material. Much of the content is drawn from David's articles and from both his and Hilary's talks to conferences. David's experience as choir director and orchestral conductor and Hilary's as singer, singing teacher and coach to choristers, is the basis for the practical advice and exercises. In the privileged position of drawing together these ideas and writing about them, Elizabeth contributes a rather different dimension. Her background in psychotherapy and education provides an additional understanding of the psychological and emotional aspects of self-expression through voice. Throughout the book, which is based upon many long and searching discussions between the three of us and the detailed checking out of the writing as it has progressed, the 'we' is truly a united voice, hopefully firmer and more authentic because of the necessity of sharing our sometimes diverse opinions and experiences.

## The approach

We address this book to choir directors and trainers of all types of choirs, including those singing in cathedrals or parish churches, colleges or primary schools, large choral societies or small local groups. Our approach is governed by the recognition that you, as choir director or trainer, whatever your background and type of choir, are motivated to learn by reflecting on your own and others' experience and are willing to try out new ideas or adapt them for your use. If it were possible, we would like to offer a dialogue through the printed page. The limitations of the published word, however, make this extremely difficult. Instead, we have adopted an interactive stance in the way the book is written, interspersing the text with questions and comments designed to stimulate you to reflect upon your own practice and experience. We urge you to regard our ideas and suggestions as opportunities to broaden your perspective on choir training and conducting and to develop the sort of self-evaluative stance to this work which is the basis for all continuing learning. Some of our suggestions may not be of use in your particular circumstances; you may disagree with some of our ideas; your own experience may lead you to different conclusions. Like all human endeavour, it is impossible to separate completely the personal and individual from the professional and task-related. Your style is your own, growing from your personality and experience. So what we suggest is not written in tablets of stone. There are few imperatives in choir directing, only the need to do as well as possible what is necessary to help your choir to give voice to the best of its capacity, and to be flexible enough to go on challenging yourself and your singers.

## The content

Singing involves physical, psychological and emotional aspects of self expression. Singing in groups, regardless of size, has the added complexities of group dynamics and social behaviour. As choir director or trainer, your main task is one of communication at many levels. We discuss this more fully later, but would like to emphasise here that your ability to communicate your intent and musical vision is central.

You are, in addition, a teacher or trainer. So, not only your musical expertise is called upon, but also in demand is your capacity to help choir members as individuals and as a corporate group to produce their voices in the most effective way to achieve your intent. This aspect of voice production, is perhaps one of the most difficult to maintain consistently over time. Each individual singer's voice production inevitably affects the quality of sound of the whole. So it is not only balance between voices and parts which comes under your jurisdiction, but also balance and resonance within each voice, enabling each choir member to recognise and develop this for themselves. The book includes many exercises which can be used to improve voice production in general to achieve a truly musical sound as well as suggestions for various musical effects.

Communication is a key concept in any group endeavour. It is especially important when the desired outcome is 'performance', in which we include liturgical singing. We explore some of the impediments to good communication with choirs and within choirs, both at rehearsal and performance stages. Ideas put forward include suggestions about conducting techniques, which are illustrated, as well as the more complex social and psychological factors.

Throughout, you will find that our common refrain is that you, the choir conductor, in the multiplicity of your tasks, are most importantly a motivator. Understanding why people come together to sing, how their enjoyment can be enhanced, and keeping up the momentum when spirits and voices are flagging, demands a high level of awareness and concentration on your part. We make suggestions about pacing rehearsals, about when to include exercises and how to use 'warm-ups', which might help you in maintaining motivation. We cannot emphasise enough, however, that knowing your choir and caring about whether or not they enjoy singing with you is basic to achieving their full participation. 'Giving voice' is, in a very fundamental way, giving something of oneself. Singers need to be confident that you value what they offer if they are to give fully of themselves through their singing.

Finally, we hope that our ideas will not only stimulate your own, but also offer support in what is essentially an isolated and sometimes lonely task. Though we consider an understanding of the singers' perspective to be important, we do not emphasise this at the cost of losing sight of the sometimes onerous responsibility of your role as choir director. However skilled and capable your choir members, they look to you as the 'leader' to enable them to produce cohesive and musical results. You are the one most likely to receive the blame when things go wrong, as well as the praise when a performance works wonders.

This book is not intended only to be read through from beginning to end. It is a handbook, something to which to refer for specific topics. The exercises in the warm-ups section may be most immediately useful to you, or understanding more about the physiology of the vocal chords, or the group dynamics operating in choirs, or the special considerations in working with very young voices. Wherever you choose to begin reading, you will find that the approach is similar. Your own experience is invaluable; reflecting upon it and building upon it is the most satisfactory outcome we could wish for in your use of this book.

# CHAPTER 1
# The Singers and the Singing

## The origins

Singing, individually or in groups is one of the most ancient forms of human expression. We cannot know for certain which came first, speaking or singing, though we assume the latter developed from the former. We can speculate about why this extension of communicating through the spoken word developed and extrapolate from similar situations in contemporary life. What differentiates the singing from the spoken voice is the extension of the range and power of sounds. This more powerful and expressive mode of vocal activity grew, perhaps, in response to the need to give voice to the otherwise emotionally inexpressible. Examples might include ululations and keening in mourning a death or the joyful whooping after success in the hunt. Singing has probably always been a way of heightening emotion, 'psyching-up' for action, as in battle-cries. We still use it as a means of calming, soothing and allaying fears, as in lullabies and the gentle instinctive crooning of mothers to very young children. Most of us are susceptible to the spontaneous 'hum', indicating quiet happiness as we potter about our business, rather like Pooh bear. Singing has, also, long been an important way of addressing the ineffable, the unspeakable because sacrosanct, connecting human beings to their spiritual sources.

It has been said that singing is a controlled form of shouting. Our contemporary imagination can easily flesh out scenarios in which our early ancestors found the value of shouting across distances too great for visual communication, part of a survival tactic which also helped them to utilise natural echoes or mimic the calls of birds and animals. Later, song was an important preservative of remembered history, and container of cultural beliefs, in mythical stories of gods and creation. The human voice, particularly when raised in song, is the most expressive instrument of all, in range, flexibility and timbre. It is our most valued means of communicating with each other. It has unique individual characteristics, which enable us to recognise each other sight unseen, as on the telephone, or from a recording. It is the most natural musical instrument and one which we all possess. Its use has been evolving for millennia. So why do we have to learn to use it? Why can we not simply sing, either individually or in groups? Why do we need a handbook to help us to help others to do what is, on one level, the most natural thing in the world?

## A gallop through history

The spontaneity of song associated with a group activity which is not primarily musical, such as we witness on newscasts of political rallies in Africa, or with football supporters in England, rugby fans in Wales, or in old sailors' work chants, suggests a deeply seated human capacity to use singing to enhance a sense of community or common effort, particularly at times of high emotion. These specially intense moments have been associated for aeons with religious experience and communal acts of worship and celebratory rites. Thus group singing moves between spontaneous outbursts of song associated with communal effort and experience and the more controlled production of group voices designed to fit into the structure and sequence of religious ceremonies. This entails a discipline and management of group singing and the necessity for trained musicians, including singers, to play a special part.

We know, from biblical and other ancient references, that large choirs were common in the Judaic ceremonies of the Temple in Jerusalem, and that the Jewish musical tradition influenced the early Christian development of liturgical music. There is evidence that in the Greek and Roman theatre, with its religious base, huge choruses of singers were trained with accompanying instrumentalists to take part in the plays. So, since ancient times, choirs have needed training, choir schools were established for this purpose, and specialists began to study voice production and to write treatises about this. The need for choir conductors and trainers became apparent. Your role is an honoured and ancient one, probably deriving from those who trained the singers and dancers in the ancient Greek paean, a choral dance to Apollo to invoke healing.

It has only been comparatively recently in our musical history that choirs have been able to extend their activities from purely religious choral works to singing for pleasure, performance and diversion. In the late middle ages, madrigals embraced secular themes, often of unrequited love (still the inspiration for many song-writers). The Renaissance courts offered special occasions when secular choral music was performed by professional musicians. The mid-eighteenth century saw the liberation of sacred choral music from the ecclesiastical setting, exemplified particularly in public performances of Handel's music.

The move to amateur voices in choirs and singing groups was encouraged by the setting up of 'clubs' for singing madrigals and in the development of societies dedicated to the preservation of old music or the encouragement of new composition. The Glee Club was founded in the 1780s, originating in England though enthusiastically adopted in North America.

Throughout the mainstream early developments in Christian choral music, most choirs consisted solely of men and boys, due to their origins in monastic tradition, though some convents also had small choirs of nuns. This male tradition continued practically unchanged until the development in the early nineteenth century of large amateur choral societies, which included women in large numbers for the first time and established the now prevalent Soprano, Alto, Tenor, Bass structure of voices. These societies sprang up in virtually every British town, emerging from political and educational movements, which believed music to be universally educative and coincided with the more general introduction of singing in the state schools. Perhaps this is where the myth began that some people can't sing, the result of lost confidence through poor teaching rather than any basic lack of ability. Everyone can sing! – though there is no doubt that some can sing better than others.[1]

Modern choirs span the range mentioned above. Their purposes are various, from the liturgical in religious ceremony to the diversionary in performance to an audience. Some choirs, as in many cathedrals, combine these functions. Choral institutions may continue the tradition of singers being only men and boys, most often the lay clerks and choristers of our great cathedral churches. There are also secular male voice choirs and 'barber shop' groups, while some cathedrals are extending their choristerships to girls. There are now many groups of women's voices. The descendants of the large mixed choral societies continue their tradition and smaller groups of mixed male and female voices spring up all the time. Some choirs are rooted in the local community, others draw from a wide area. Some specialise in a particular style or period of music, others are eclectic in their range. The sheer amount of music currently available to choirs is mind-boggling, and new compositions appear regularly.

Members may be young children or adults or a mixture of both. They may be completely amateur, semi-professional or dedicatedly professional singers, reflecting their ability to read music and produce their voices well. Choirs may consist of a few voices or extend their membership to more than a hundred. Their members may meet regularly and frequently, or occasionally. Membership may remain fairly static or change fairly rapidly, as in choirs associated with colleges or schools. The list of variables seems inexhaustible – you can probably think of more from your own experience. Whatever the mix 'n match of these characteristics, each combination of purpose, membership and musical predilection will affect how the choir performs and the specific help required from the director to perform better.

---

Reflect upon your own choir – what are its purposes in meeting? What is its composition? How stable is its membership? How competent is its musical ability? How well do its members produce their voices? What would you like to change about it? With what are you content?

---

The common denominator is that of the *communion of singing*. Its most obvious context is the 'communion' of religious ceremony and service to God. But people also come together to sing because it pleases them to make vocal music with others; because the jointness of the effort is important and satisfying; because this is a cherished opportunity to sing regularly; because they love exercising that most subtle and flexible of musical instruments, the voice. Your facilitation of this communion is as much a privilege as it is a responsibility.

# CHAPTER 2
# The Voice

## The alchemy of singing

Alchemy was the science and art of transformation, either of base metal into gold, or, symbolically at a philosophical level, of the disparate parts of a person into an integrated self. Cherry Gilchrist, a singer and voice teacher, has written:

'Singing is one of the most intimate forms of alchemy that we can ever experience. In the twinkling of an eye, we transform air into sound. Our body itself is the alchemist's vessel; we breathe air into it and transmute the air into musical sound on the outflow . . . But what I would call the real alchemy of singing starts when a person begins to work consciously upon his or her voice. Then that seed potential can be developed into something greater, a voice with more power and range, but, above all, one that is truly expressive. Our aim in singing is then a higher form of transmutation whereby we are capable of turning an emotional impulse directly into sound.'[1]

The voice, then, is the instrument of the whole person, with physical, psychological and emotional components contributing to its production. We bring body, mind and feeling to the act of singing. Indeed, speaking voices quickly reveal in the quality of their vibrancy and resonance a great deal about how the speaker is. We soon perceive when physical energy is low or spirits down from a short conversation. We recognise confidence and well-being from the ring of the spoken word. We know what effort goes into projecting speech to a large group and how easily nervousness can disrupt breathing and sabotage the spoken voice. How much more so, then, in singing, when we extend the use of our vocal instrument.

There are many, sometimes conflicting, theories as to the best way to go about combining the physical, mental and emotional aspects of voice production. Papers are extant which were written for choir schools and singing teachers in the middle ages. One of the earliest attempts at devising a complete singing method was made by the physiologist Giovanni Camilio Maffei in 1562, in his *Discorso della voce del modo d'apparare de cantar di garganta*, a 'self-help' manual for singers. Later texts also emphasised the value of understanding the complexity of the physical aspects of the 'instrument', including the importance of breathing and posture, as in *Le traité complet de l'art du chant* (1840) by Manuel Garcia, who taught Jenny Lind. This 'scientific' and analytical approach continued to be developed into the early part of this century, but later fell foul of more 'holistic' theories which regarded voice production as more intuitive, as in Judith Litante's book *A Natural Approach to Singing* (1962).[2]

There are many who have influenced our thinking and practice. Of particular interest, and because his book is now out of print, is Henry Coward's *Choral Technique and Interpretation*,[3] which emphasises the importance of vocal training for choirs. He was for many years the conductor of the Sheffield Choral Society and we quote him at some length for his insights into choir training. He employed an enthusiastic and peculiarly Edwardian style of expression, which is a foil for our own approach.

We recognise the value of understanding the components of voice production – the 'analytical' approach, but also share the view that the intuitive approach to singing as a natural form of self expression is important. The following discussion starts analytically, breaking down and describing the physical aspects of voice production, but concludes holistically, considering the necessary integration of the physical, psychological and emotional in singing.

---

What is your view? What aspect do you consider most important in voice production? How do you experience the connection between individual voice production and choral technique as a whole?

---

## The physiology of singing

'Singers should not produce musical tones with a voice gaping wide in a distorted fashion or with an absurdly powerful bellowing, especially when singing at the divine mysteries; moreover, they should avoid tones having a wide and ringing vibrato, since these tones do not maintain a true pitch and because of their continuous wobble cannot form a balanced concord with other voices.'

You would probably agree with this comment from Gaffurius in his treatise *Practica Musica* (1496).[4] Henry Coward refers to the harsh harmonics which occur when voices are not produced well, affecting the homogeneity of choral sound.[5] He emphasises the importance of singers understanding why and how the placing of the voice affects both its individual sound and the balance of voices in the choir. This means that choir trainers must also be aware of how the voice works and how to correct its poor production.

---

How much do you know about the actual physiology of voice? Do you sing yourself and have first hand practice in exercises to improve voice production? How aware are you of the actual physical sensations of singing and the difference in these sensations between 'good' and 'bad' voice production? How aware are your singers of these things?

---

## The mechanics of the voice

Sound is produced by air passing over the vocal chords (larynx) and resonating in various chambers of the body. That is the simple explanation of a simple act! We do it all the time without thinking about it, a purely intuitive physical exercise. Artistic singing, however, makes us aware of the complexity of the mechanics involved, when we strive for particular musical effects. The aim, in the long run, is to help your singers develop techniques so that the sound they produce appears natural and unforced. This involves making them conscious of physical activities which normally operate unconsciously. While it is generally accepted that, regardless of innate ability, all instrumentalists need practised technique in order to produce fluent music, it is not so widely accepted among amateur groups that singing demands a similar approach.

Like any musical instrument, the voice needs a supply of power, a tone producer and regulator and resonators. The power supply is the breath, the tone producer and regulator is the larynx and the resonators are all the bony cavities of our bodies. Controlling the interaction of all three is the secret to harmonious singing.[6]

## The larynx

We start with the larynx as central to voice production. It is tiny – approximately 15 mm long in adults and 11mm in young choristers. It works as a valve to hold breath and to prevent foreign bodies entering the lungs as it sits at the top of the windpipe (trachea). Despite its smallness, it is an immensely strong combination of cartilege, muscle and ligaments, with a complex set of connections to surrounding tissue. Looked at in cross section from above, its shape appropriately resembles an Apollonian harp.

We do not intend to go into the fine detail of its working here, but suggest that you ensure that your singers are at least somewhat aware of its site, complexity and function. Of particular importance in understanding tone production and regulation, is the knowledge that not only its internal but also its external muscular connections are significant, as this involves consideration of throat and facial musculature as well as posture. It is one of the strongest yet most flexible organs we possess. Alerting your singers to these characteristics may help to make them more confident in its use.

The vocal folds produce sound, when they are pulled together by a lowering of pressure along their edges before being pushed apart by a difference in air pressure across the glottis which leads to a rapid series of puffs of air passing through them. This is what happens with our vocal folds and breath each time we change tonal quality.

The attack of a vowel sound is, therefore, a combination of muscular adjustment and the action of the breath. The effect initiated by suction is different from that which occurs when air is forced through closed vocal folds, which is generally thought to be unhealthy for the larynx, and is designated *coup de glotte*, because of the increased tension on the vocal chords striking together. We suggest exercises for vocal well-being later, but here would mention that, especially when practising an attack on a high note, it is advisable to avoid the *coup de glotte* by allowing some breath to escape and therefore relaxing the vocal chords before 'giving voice'.

## Registers within the larynx

While there is an important relationship to do with voice register between the larynx and its resonators, it is generally accepted that the changes of register are substantially within the larynx, rather than outside it. Most singers would acknowledge in themselves a distinction between a 'heavy' and a 'light' register, though experts have disagreed as to the number of registers in the voice. The need to move smoothly between them is the cause of some difficulty, because the singer is so aware of the different sensations related to the different quality of sound. The bottom of the voice generally feels 'heavy', the sensation lightening as the voice ascends. At some place in the middle there is a combination effect. Labels, which might not always seem helpful, have been tagged to three main registers, referring to the resonators, in a woman, of chest, middle, head and, in a man, of chest, head, falsetto. Some writers refer to the notion of *passagio* as the threshold in the larynx that leads from one register to another, suggesting that the mechanics of the vocal chords change dramatically at each turning point. Some singers speak of actually feeling the chords behave differently, and imagine them opening in different ways in different registers. The images which help singers to 'see' this essentially unconscious and intuitive action are varied. For some, imagining the 'voice' being pulled back to a focal point, rather like a catapult, before being released and projected, is a helpful image.

There are strong psychological and learned influences on how singers experience the 'entrance' into a different register, often leading to artificially produced sounds. This is particularly significant in achieving high notes and in the case of young voices, when boys may be pushed into producing chest voices, creating later problems and the false diagnosis that the voice has 'broken'. The terminology referring to a voice 'breaking' and the expectation it elicits of potential problems and loss of vocal ability, suggests pathology in what should be a perfectly normal developmental change. Of course, abusing a boy's voice by, for example, forcing him to sing upward scales beyond a comfortable range can also produce artificial 'breaks'. The falling vocal register of pubescent boys indicates a natural hormonal change, not generally a 'broken' voice, unless there is medical evidence, such as nodes, to support this. Upward scales and exercises, taught incorrectly, are often the cause of breaks from middle to head voice. Fostering the sensation of 'being above' one's voice, looking down on it, can help singers of all ages to avoid difficulties in changing registers.

---

Ask your choir whether they attach any particular images to the internal sensations of the voice moving through different registers.

---

## Resonance

It is important for singers to *see* the voice in the round, even though it appears at any one time to be operating in one mode, for example 'head' or 'chest'. It actually makes use of all the resonators available in the body, though one may be dominant to achieve a particular note or effect. One of the most difficult skills lies in combining, to the best effect demanded by the music, the range of resonating cavities available. Thinking of the voice as having a centre of gravity, or being centred, can assist singers to make full use of their range without fear of wobbling off the note.

There is an intrinsic connection between the use of particular resonators and the shape and action of the larynx, though the exact mechanisms are poorly understood. Though the bony cavities of chest and head, as we suggest above, are significant (psychologically as well as physically), the most important resonator is generally believed to be the pharynx. This may be thought of as the voice's 'centre'. 'Open-throat' singing has become a sine qua non of pedagogical approaches. Although it is much talked about, it is not so clearly understood in practice. Exercises to encourage singing with open throat are suggested later. Here it is important to understand why this seems a favourable method. Henry Coward, in trying to rid his singers of harsh harmonics, aimed for 'nasal resonance', not, we hasten to add, a 'nasal sound', but implying openness at the back of the throat, enlarging the pharynx as in a yawn and using the connection to the sinus cavities. This reinforces the lower overtones, giving the voice a mellow quality. The pitch of the pharynx has been estimated at between 350 and 750 Hz, a range in which the singer can adjust tone quality to fit the music.

Yawning, or the sensation of doing so, has been used as an exercise towards achieving an open throat for many years. What is equally important is the position of the tongue. If the tongue is up it constricts the throat space; if down and firmly anchored behind the front bottom teeth, it allows the space to enlarge both in the pharynx and the mouth. Breathing deeply and silently also helps to achieve this tongue-relaxed position. An additional mechanism in promoting open throatedness is in the raising of the soft palate, again as in yawning. When this upward stretch is well co-ordinated with the downward stretch, there is a strengthening of harmonics in the upper range. There is an important high frequency, around 2,800 Hz, which lends intensity of 'ring' to voices. This resonance can be maintained, once learned, whether the music be soft or loud, and is often felt acutely in the frontal areas of the face and nasal cavities. It is also known as 'forward resonance'. Interestingly, it is suggested that while the singer may feel an intensification of resonance on deliberately opening up the nasal and sinus cavities, audiences do not necessarily appreciate the change in vocal tone. This is an important aspect of learning to produce voice, the fact that what is heard and sensed in the singer's body, and heard in the head especially, is not necessarily what is experienced by the listener.

Projection and focus of voice enter the discussion here, and these involve serious psychological considerations, which are explored later. A useful metaphor is that of light in the camera and depth of field. The focus, or sharpness of projection, is increased in length the smaller the aperture; the focus falls off in length, producing a soft and fuzzy image, when the apperture is enlarged. The voice, likewise, needs intensity, not loudness, to be properly focused and projected. Apparent loudness does not enhance clarity.

## Breathing

Some claim that this is the most important aspect of singing; others that it should be regarded as a natural function, which will occur spontaneously as the singer recognises what is happening in the voice. We suggest that both approaches have virtue. The breath is the energy, the power which fuels the voice. Though there may seem to be a difference between the 'fuel' needed for speaking and that for singing, it is not as great as is usually taught. It is not so much the amount of breath, as the muscles of support, the intercostals and the diaphragm, which regulate the supply of breath to the vocal chords which are important. Hilary recalls a singing teacher, Laura Sarti, saying 'You need only take in as much air as a rose takes – it's how you control it that matters.' In our view, 'deep breathing' does not mean over-breathing, with great gulps of air, which often happens when choir conductors mouth 'Breathe!' at their singers. Rather it means to feel as though the breath is coming from a deep place, the abdomen, because this is where the muscles of support are. Over-emphasis on the diaphragm and 'deep breathing' can lead to tension in the body and a breathy sound. A relaxed breath feels natural, is quiet and provides a greater reserve.

Breathing for singing, therefore, is straightforward in that it is natural, but difficult, in that it has to be co-ordinated and controlled in relation to what is happening in the vocal chords. The freedom of movement of the breath is one of the most important aspects, and this is related to body posture and to relaxation. Relaxation has psychological components, as does breath control, which we shall address later.

From a purely physical point of view, correct posture is crucial to free breathing. Though once the idea of posture has been grasped, singers find the way of breathing for singing in any posture, as can be seen from opera. Like most 'rules', once mastered, one can relinquish its ordinances, as the discipline becomes internalised.

The correct stance (see Fig 1) epitomises the combination of relaxation and discipline necessary in so many of the other aspects of singing. The head should be relaxed and erect, as if suspended on a thread; the chest should be reasonably high, with shoulders relaxed and arms hanging by the sides; the back of the neck should feel stretched and lengthened; the pelvis should be tilted forward slightly, the rear pulled downwards; the feet should be well-planted, with weight evenly distributed and a sense of being grounded, yet ready for action. Some teachers find the Alexander technique useful in achieving this.

Breathing should be silent and felt deeply, expanding the lower ribs while the diaphragm descends enlarging the thorax. The sternum, raised slightly, should not drop as the breath is exhaled in order to vocalise, while the abdominal muscles contract to meet the resistance of the intercostals and diaphragm (see Fig 2). Figures 3 and 4 show what happens to the hands when placed before breathing in and after.

When described like this, breathing for singing can appear to be so contrived and self-conscious as to provide an impediment, not an aid. It is, therefore, important, while helping your singers to understand the importance of useful breathing, to ensure that the exercises you offer them to improve this aspect of voice production are completely linked to voice practice, so that breathing becomes natural not artificial. Managing the flow of breath over the vocal chords is the aim, not teaching people to breathe for life. For this reason and because each person has a different way of connecting breathing to voice, it is generally not helpful to say "Breathe !" to everyone at the beginning of pieces or phrases. We suggest some breathing awareness exercises later, in the section on warm-ups.

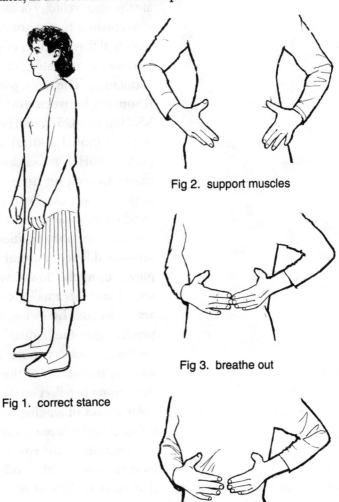

Fig 1. correct stance

Fig 2. support muscles

Fig 3. breathe out

Fig 4. breathe in

## Diction

Enunciation in speech and in singing often needs to be different if the singing voice is properly produced. Vowels are of particular importance in achieving resonance. Consonants, necessary for the intelligibility of words, can inhibit resonance, by, for instance, putting the tongue in a position which precludes an open throat. The characteristics of consonants are as wide ranging as the ways of producing them. It is not our intention here to enter into a detailed description of their impact on singing.[7] Suffice it to suggest that singers may have to learn how to pronounce words differently while singing, and still achieve comprehensibility. Exercises to improve enunciation in singing are suggested later, but it might be helpful here to offer some simple explanations about the effects of vowels on voice, since they are the main vehicles of sound.

According to our source each vowel sound demands a slightly different action of the larynx and has a characteristic frequency consisting of a fundamental tone and related harmonics.[8] The range goes from *oo* at the lower end, which resonates between 400 and 800 Hz, through *oh* (500-850Hz), *ah* (825-1,200Hz), *a* – as in c*a*t (750-1,800Hz), *e* – as in g*e*t (550-1,900Hz), *a* – as in c*a*ge (550-2,100Hz), *ee* (375-2,400Hz). It can easily be seen why certain vowels are easier to sing on high notes, because of their natural frequency range, and why singers are therefore told to convert to others to achieve resonance. Singers can learn to combine the characteristic qualities of sound of different vowels to produce different musical effects. For instance, practising a phrase using the 'lower' vowels, such as *oo*, can darken the sound and this quality can be retained in performing the actual words. Likewise, brightening can be achieved by practising to the 'lighter' or 'higher' vowel sounds. Such exercises involve a strong element of imagination about the interior sensations of the singer in producing voice, and move us on to reflect on the psychological aspects of singing.

An aspect of singing which provides a bridge into that rather complex arena is vibrato. This is a fluctuation in pitch and intensity of the voice, and can be as much as a tone in loud singing. Unlike Gaffurius[9], modern scholars suggest that there is little or no connection between vibrato and intonation, though there is fluctuation in intensity. The listener tends to hear an average of the two outer limits of the vibrato. The frequency of vibrato in a trained voice is about seven per second, though this generally varies with the emotional intensity of the music and the emotional state of the singer. The vibrato is what lends colour to the voice, and is often cultivated to achieve particular effects in certain types of singing. The slower the vibrato the 'heavier' the sound. Singing without vibrato can only be achieved by decreasing activity in the muscles involved in the working of the larynx and reducing the energy of the breath. It is clear that such singing also demands a diminished emotional response in the singer, since, willy-nilly, our emotions are expressed through our voices. This is a good point, then, to move into the psychology of singing.

---

Before doing so, we suggest that you reflect on what we have written about the physiology of voice and think about how much it might help to explain some of it to your singers. If you are working with young children such learning about themselves can be fun. For adults it can help to root their increased confidence and capacity to sing in the ground of shared understanding. Perhaps a diagram would assist them to understand more about how they 'give voice'? Do you consider it important to explain why as well as how your choir should do exercises to improve voice production?

---

We suggest that even young children can benefit from the understanding that comes from repeatedly putting concepts into practice, slowly incorporating them so that they become second nature. Most important, for all singers, is the appreciation that the voice is the instrument of the whole body and that singing is at the same time the most simple, because the most natural, yet the most complex act of self expression.

# CHAPTER 3
# The Psychology of Singing

## The individual

The word 'psychology' seems to enter every domain these days, and you may read it with some aversion, thinking that you are being asked to navel-gaze or analyse behaviour in a way that is inappropriate to your task as musician. It might help to remember that you are, as choir director, a trainer as well as a facilitator of group interaction, albeit of a highly specialised nature.

We have pointed out already how the emotional state of the singer affects the sound of the voice, influencing its fluency, intensity and vibrato. It hardly needs saying then that the psychology of singing is the psychology of self expression. It not only involves confidence and concentration in producing the voice, but also the ability to enter into the nature of the music being sung. We could call this entering the soul of the music. 'Psyche' comes from the Greek, meaning soul, spirit or mind. This suggests that singers should be able to use imagination to connect with and express the music as well as to better understand the workings of the voice. Many of the exercises we suggest later are designed to enhance the ability of singers to enter into the processes of singing by visualising what is happening in their bodies. This is the place where mind and body most completely connect, the 'alchemy' of singing. Your ability to communicate a vision of what a piece of music conveys to you is a crucial bridge for the choir in jointly imagining themselves into the music.

Most people are not encouraged to use their imaginations after school-age, or to think about 'soul' out of a religious context. It might be more helpful to think about the 'essence' of the sound. It is important to remember that people are not free to use their imagination if they are feeling restricted by anxiety or lack confidence due to the fear of criticism for 'getting it wrong' – a scenario too often associated for adults (and children) with unhappy memories of school. To use imagination in singing, to 'give voice' openly means that sometimes it will be with wrong notes, poor intonation, mistaken timing, depending on the characteristics and abilities of the choir. To learn is to have the freedom to make mistakes, and choral singing is about learning to sing together.

## The group

How people feel about themselves and others engaged in a joint endeavour inevitably affects how they behave, or perform. Choral singing is a group activity of the utmost intensity and, often, complexity, in which the whole is greater than the sum of its parts, but in which a few 'off-key' parts can wreak havoc. Singers must co-operate with each other, listen to each other, feel reasonably comfortable with each other and therefore confident to 'give voice' in what is often a demanding and critical context. Singing, as we have said earlier, is self expression, easily encouraged or impeded by the atmosphere in which it takes place. Many people join choirs for social, as well as musical, reasons. In large choirs it may be difficult to get to know people; even in small choirs attention may not be given to this aspect of interaction.

Workers with groups convened for other purposes have long known that the group dynamic is an essential feature of any joint activity, and that it must be nurtured at the beginning of each group encounter to ensure that it works for, not against, the group enterprise. This does not mean lengthy how-de-dos and how-are-yous, but it does suggest that, as director, you have an opportunity to acknowledge, in your own way, at the beginning of each rehearsal, that it matters to you how people are feeling together, not least because this will affect how they will sing together.

It may not be a matter of unfamiliarity with each other, so much as over-familiarity, as in some school or church choirs, which leads to discomfort and therefore inhibited singing, the sort of unrelaxed attitudes which tighten throat, affect breathing and induce tension. You can probably think of examples of this from your own experience, where other agendas are brought into the choir and sabotage the group effort in making music.

We are not suggesting that as choir director you are responsible for the singers' well-being outside the choir, only that it may be very helpful to you to be aware of potential 'social' hazards which will affect your choir's singing. In any case, remembering to 'warm-up' the choir socially, by your initial attitude, can be effectively enhanced by using exercises which will induce relaxation, cohesion and confidence. They need take only a few moments at the beginning of each rehearsal. We offer some suggestions and exercises later. Try them, amend them, embellish them, according to your own personality and style and the needs of the choir, or invent your own.

## Selecting the singers

Henry Coward said that people commented on the quality of voices in his choir, assuming that he chose only the best and most musical. This was far from the reality for him and probably for most choir directors who must 'make do' with the mixture of voices, from good to indifferent, which their choir members possess. The urge to sing does not necessarily provide the singer with an exquisite or refined instrument, though it probably does assume the enthusiasm to learn to improve its use. Coward even suggested that he preferred to work with basically untrained voices which he could then mould into a homogeneous, though not uniform, sound. So what do we seek or hope for in choir members' ability to sing?

---

Reflect on your own choir, and ask yourself what it is you most enjoy about their voices. If you could start from scratch, what sort of singers would you take on? What do you look for when you audition new aspirants for membership?

---

David Hill says of choristers:

'My aim as a choir master is for the voices to resonate. At Westminster some people thought the choir had a "shouty tone", but George Malcolm's famous phrase, that "good singing is a controlled form of shouting" is absolutely true; if you listen to children playing in a playground they don't shout to each other in an insipid head-voice; they use strong, naturally produced resonant chest sound. If you have the same objective for boys' singing voices they begin to sound like their adult counterparts. A large acoustic can do a lot of work for a choir but ultimately that doesn't solve anything. A well-produced sound in a resonant building will still sound well in a dry acoustic . . .'[1]

In choristers, he looks for boys, from seven to nine years of age, who have good and clear voices, a good and responsive ear, a bright and intelligent character and enthusiasm about the prospect of being a chorister.

Directors of cathedral choirs are in a privileged position as, generally, there is considerable competition to become a chorister. But their view of the sort of voice and attitude they seek is not dissimilar to that of Henry Coward, who hoped for adult voices which were fairly powerful, properly produced, agile and flexible and controlled. He did not always expect to find them. This is the ground from which voice training can grow, to produce a collectively harmonious choir sound. You, as trainer, have to create from what Coward called a 'feeble germ' the elements which make good singing possible, which demands sensitivity and patience.

David Hill makes much the same comment about young people's voices, though he suggests that the difference in physical size of both children and their vocal chords must be borne in mind in their development. He adds:

'Too much of one type of voice and insufficient of another are common faults in choirs . . . It is foolish of a choir master to think that in every choir all the boys are potentially soloists. Some may have better voices than others, even though one has chosen them all because they have a basic ability to sing. Some end up singing better than others. Perhaps the single, most important aspect of choir training is to have some idea of the sound that you are ultimately trying to get from the entire choir; you have to have a vision of what you are trying to achieve. The sound will change, of course, depending upon who is in the choir ; the sound can't remain the same year in and year out if the personnel change. If it does sound the same then there is something wrong. The notion of getting all the boys to sound the same as each other is incorrect; the object is to get a naturally produced sound, so that then one can bring individuals together to create a particular sound and a particular balance within that sound; if they are blending a false sound, or one which is inhibited because it is being held back, then a choir master might create sounds which are quite nice to listen to, but unfortunately he may damage the singers' voices as result . . .

Choir trainers are in a privileged, and rather precarious, position, in that we are custodians of people's voices and we must be careful to treat them properly.'[2]

We return to the questions about warming-up the voice and proper exercises for voice training, implicit in the above, in later sections. Even in choirs which contain professional singers, similar issues arise. The production of a balanced and particular sound, relating to your vision of what is appropriate for the choir and the music being performed, is the central quest.

It is relevant here to mention, in general terms, the relationship of repertoire to the sort of voices you may be seeking. Detailed discussion of this topic is outside the scope of this book, but we would suggest that you consider well the appropriateness of particular pieces of music to the capabilities of your choir members as well as to the context in which they sing. This means not only reflecting on their skills and the demands of the repertoire and on how long you have to practise, but also on the music's suitability in terms of the purposes of the choir. Though it can be exciting to help choirs to achieve results in repertoire which they at first may consider 'too difficult', it can also be disillusioning if you have tried to push them beyond their capacity to perform well. Likewise, people tend not to sing well if they remain untouched by or dislike the music selected for them, or feel it to be inappropriate to the occasion of performance. If you want to try something which is rather different from, or more difficult than, your choir's usual programme, you may have to do some 'educational' work with them. You are likely to carry them with you more enthusiastically, if you can share your interest in the particular piece and explain its place in choral music. Listening together to a recorded performance can assist in this process of familiarisation.

# CHAPTER 4
# The Choir Director

## Background and training

At last we come specifically to you. Here we should dissociate ourselves from any implied sexism in quotes and comments. We recognise that many of you reading this book are women. In our view, 'choir director' has no implicit gender and refers to both sexes. It needs to be acknowledged, however, that for many working in ecclesiastical settings, the reality is that both the structure of the church and the gender of its servants is largely masculine. This is not the place or the book to enter into a fuller exploration of gender issues. We simply want to acknowledge them and to avoid inadvertently offending any of our readers.

There is a rich diversity of those for whom the designation 'choir director/trainer' is appropriate, in terms of experience, background and motivation. While there may be common ground in musical expertise, there can be no absolute standards applicable to everyone in this role.

---

We would like to ask you to reflect upon what, if any, training you have had in the direction and training of choirs? What would you have liked to have had? What opportunities can you look forward to now?

---

You may have been fortunate and have had special teaching in choir-training. If so, you are in the minority amongst your colleagues. It appears that most choir directors pick up the tools of their trade and the skills to use them in a rather hit-and-miss fashion. With luck, learning from the experience of participating as a choir member with a good director, will have laid some solid foundations upon which to build your own style and practice. The general assumption seems to be that if you are a graduate of a college of music, particularly if you are an organist, you automatically know about choir training and directing. David Hill comments on his own early experience:

'My first attempts with choirs were less than distinguished. I remember as an ambitious thirteen year-old at music school in Manchester, that if the choir I was conducting sang flat or the ensemble was far from precise, then it must have been their fault, since 'my beat was perfectly clear', or 'flat singing was due to the singers not listening to each other'; and ' what have those faults got to do with me?' It may have been that both reasons were feasible, but perhaps there was only a grain of truth in the excuses presented. What was clearer than anything else was my lack of technique in all areas of direction, and only when a new director of music arrived at Chetham's, Michael Brewer, did I realise how little I knew about choir training. His whole approach was to convey the importance of technique in order to produce a controlled and musical result. He made us sing lots of exercises to improve our vocal range, breathing and so on, and then incorporated those ideas within the choir rehearsals. All this was new to me, and I found it particularly intriguing. Many of the things I consider to be important now are a result of that earlier experience.'[1]

Learning from one's own experience, as conductor and choral singer, is a point of view shared by Henry Coward[2] whose insights were not only based upon years of conducting a large mixed-voice choir, but also stemmed from his own experience of singing and practising the exercises he gave to his singers. This he considered to be an important aspect of working with choirs.

## Motivation

This is a key word. Your ability to motivate your choir depends upon your own motivation to be a choir director. Your enthusiasm will engage their eagerness to learn to produce a good sound. Before we get into more detailed discussion of what makes a 'good' choir conductor, we suggest that you ask yourself:

---

Why do I do it? Is it part of my general music responsibilities, as church organist or music teacher, for instance? Do I enjoy this part of my work? Do I think I do it well? What would I like to do better? Is it a purely voluntary activity? What in my own musical training has enabled me to conduct a choir? What can I translate from my musical background into my work as choir conductor?

---

It would be presumptuous to suggest that there is only one way to conduct a choir, or that there are ten golden rules which, if obeyed, will lead to perfection. We want to emphasise that ours is not a counsel of *perfection;* there are no *ideal* choir directors or trainers; there are only those who want to learn to be better at what is a difficult task in the service of making wonderful and satisfying music for listeners and singers alike, not to mention themselves. Everyone brings their own personality, experience and particular style to the process of motivating choirs to produce musical sounds. But learning to sustain a choir's and your own motivation is central to the task. It has many facets and involves many aspects of individual and group behaviour, some of which are infrequently addressed and perhaps poorly understood.

Your attitude and self-discipline are the most influential in maintaining the fine balance between encouragement and coercion of your singers. The old educational adage, that people do well when they are expected to, is a useful guideline. Aiming to achieve slightly more than your singers believe possible can be an effective motivator, so long as you do not over-estimate to the point of disillusion. This may seem a difficult balance at times, but music itself comes to your aid, and the magic of making it together with others.

We break down 'choir conducting' into some of its constituent parts in the sections which follow. As a precursor to our suggestions about making it more manageable, we emphasise the overall importance of your relationship with the choir and its manifestation. David Hill comments:

'One of the hardest things for any choirmaster, particularly the more introverted among us, is to project a seemingly unending amount of confidence, personality and general "bonhomie" . . . But it would be all too easy for any of us, in creating the respect which is necessary, to resort to sarcasm or to allowing our egos to inflate, so that we become pompous and overbearing.'[3]

This surely applies, whatever the age and ability of your choir members, and however frayed nerves and tempers may become. The wise choir director remembers never to treat adults like children and generally to treat children like adults – at least when making music. Whatever your style and however you begin work on particular pieces of music, the first fifteen minutes of your interaction with the choir will set the tone for the remainder and will determine whether or not it is productive and enjoyable for all of you. David Hill has invented a diagram to express his view of the importance of motivating a choir:

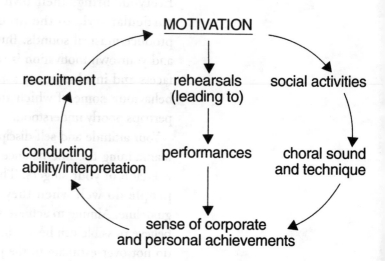

He emphasises the value of relating to choir members in a lively and friendly manner, but warns against too laissez-faire an approach, which can lead to sloppy and flat singing and lack of respect for the conductor. He comments, 'The conductor who occasionally raises the voice and sounds irritated has a far more dramatic and longlasting effect than the director who uses a temper as a modus operandi.'

We suggest that you ask yourself the following questions to determine your own approach:

---

When I begin a rehearsal, how do I start my interaction with choir members? How have I prepared for what we are about to do? How much do I know about my choir and their expectations? Am I clear about my expectations of them? If so, how do I express these?

---

Reflecting on your answers may help you to spot areas of difficulty as well as things that you feel work well. We offer some ideas which may be useful in deciding how to progress your work with your choir.

## Preparation and planning
### Administration

A surprisingly large amount of planning in advance goes into successful choir direction and the maintenance of a choir's commitment. Quiet and unpretentious efficiency in preparing and circulating a choir's diary at the beginning of the year, including performance dates and what will be rehearsed when, is usually much appreciated by choir members, as well as being helpful to you. Not that such a timetable should be inflexible, but it does give a sense of purpose to the singers as well as the idea that you are clear what you are about. It also offers choir members the opportunity to learn new, or brush up on old, pieces of music at a particular time. This may be an easier and more obvious aid in church choirs, which are governed by the demands of the liturgical calendar. When producing such diaries, it is essential that they should be typewritten and clearly photocopied. They may also need to be negotiated in some aspects with choir members, particularly if they or their representatives on a committee have a say in music to be performed.

The agreed timetable should also be clear about start and finish times, which you would be advised to adhere to as strictly as humanly possible. Nothing is more annoying or damaging to morale and motivation than a choir director who is often late, or frequently sends a substitute at short notice. Building an effective relationship with your choir, in which your commitment mirrors their own, cannot be achieved in absentia. On the other hand, sympathy with the travelling problems of some singers will be well received and help them to be more relaxed about your own unavoidable difficulties in arriving on time or, occasionally, at all. If you cannot be there yourself, either make sure that your substitute really knows what s/he is doing or cancel the rehearsal.

Planning also involves ensuring that suitable premises are available for rehearsals on a regular basis, and that they are well supplied with air in the summer and heat in the winter, as well as sufficient room for the number of singers. It is surprising how many choirs have to make do with inadequate facilities, which again can have the effect of decreasing motivation to attend rehearsals. These matters may seem to be out of your hands; even so, it is helpful to listen to any complaints that may arise sympathetically and not to dismiss them out of hand because you feel helpless to change arrangements.

There may be other administrative matters which preoccupy you due to specific circumstances. We suggest you try to address these specifically, if possible before the year's rehearsals begin, so that work with the choir can start as smoothly as possible.

## Music

The preparation of music requires personal study of the work before the first rehearsal, and possibly the need to make amendments to the schedule as the rehearsals continue and specific difficulties arise. Choirs have reason to be critical of conductors who appear not to have prepared their scores beforehand; in addition, the more prepared you feel, the greater will be your confidence and the more impact you will have on your singers.

There are several main steps which can assist in preparing a score. These are:

• Play the work through on the piano to ensure that you know it well – this will also help you to study the harmony and its direction, which is vital in indicating key parts, words or phrases when conducting.

• Indicate breath marks in all vocal parts – these may be changed later, but an initial idea of the shape and outline of the music will emerge and you will be able to sing through the various parts to anticipate likely problems.

• Mark in the dynamics – even though these may already be supplied by the composer; this will help to familiarise you with the overall shape of dynamic levels and contrasts. Each phrase needs consideration and you should not be afraid of changing editorial markings, as long as you have clear and strong reasons.

• Anticipate problems of intonation – by marking notes which are likely to be problematic, either from a musical or pronunciation point of view, with up or downward pointing arrows.

• Underline important syllables and words – which carry the sense of the text as well as govern the musical phrase, while avoiding exaggerated phrasing which will upset the overall architecture and legato line of the piece.

• Select the most appropriate tempo – this is likely to be the most difficult task so we give it wider coverage. There are several factors which should be considered when deciding upon the tempo, some of which are governed by your personal choice. It is sensible to start with the most obvious, the editorial marking on the score – 'adagio', 'andante', 'allegro' etc. Secondly, how you experience the mood of the music will affect your decision. Thirdly, a sense of the tempo appropriate to the style of the music and to the capabilities of your choir is important. Each musical piece has its own intrinsic pulse, so the tempo must take account of this and encourage the flow of the music. Finally, the acoustic in which the music will be sung will influence your choice. Some believe that in a reverberant acoustic, not slowing the tempo overall, but giving extra time at the end of phrases coupled with clear articulation in the faster moments, allows detail to be heard. However, there is a case for easing tempi in reverberant acoustics and quickening them in more difficult 'drier' acoustics. Easing the tempo allows the singers, assisted by the acoustic, to feel and sound relaxed, offers greater flexibility to mould the musical phrases, and produces a more intense performance. The less responsive and 'drier' acoustic generally demands the opposite approach to millitate against fatigue in the singers; slightly brisker tempi seem to work better. We emphasise that the characteristics of different acoustics should only result in *slight* changes of tempi, because any radical departure from what has been practised can not only upset the choir but may also call into question your musical integrity. As a practical summary we give overleaf an analysis by David Hill of the first eight bars of Bruckner's wonderful motet *Locus iste* 'This place was made by God'.[4]

## A practical summary – Locus iste

**Bar 1:** *Allegro moderato* – this poses the first problem. Obviously, it means 'moderately fast', but anything too quick would be facile and lacking in reverence, but treated as an *Adagio* (as it often is), the music fails to reflect the mood or text of the motet. Therefore I would suggest a speed of ♩ = 80 - 100 would be acceptable.

Listen to the soprano and bass C; they must be in tune with each other. If you are unhappy about the sound of the first chord, remove altos and tenors in order to listen to the basses and sopranos.

Repeated notes (altos and basses) must not lower in pitch and the soprano phrase needs careful tuning as it descends.

The shape of the musical phrase needs very subtle treatment. A *crescendo* (only small) from Bar 1 to 2 with a *diminuendo* during the 'iste', linked to a growth in intensity within the phrase, should create the right effect.

**Bar 2:** You may wish to shorten the third crotchet of bar 2 to make way for the bass lead 'a Deo'. I would suggest a link in bar 2 and a small *crescendo* between the second and third bar for the basses. Rehearse them separately in this.

**Bar 3:** Word stress is important here, avoiding 'a Deo'. The sense of line (= legato) will need explanation and that the phrase must aim towards bar 4, but with only a small amount of *crescendo,* say *p* to *mp*.

**Bar 4:** A gradual *diminuendo* and placing together of 'est' on the final crotchet rest.

**Bars 5-8:** These require the same treatment as bars 1-4, but with a stronger dynamic level: *mf* to *f*.

Two other points to consider: how quietly can your choir take a breath? Ideally, the breathing should be inaudible, though this is difficult to achieve. Teach them to inhale slowly, and never to take the breath just prior to singing.

Finally, proper pronunciation of the Latin should help to produce a resonant, blended sound, and here are a few guidelines for consideration:

Locus – 'Lo' as in l*o*st

iste – 'is' as in *ea*sy

a – as in *A*frica not *a*wful

Deo – 'De' as in d*e*nt; 'o' as in l*o*st and not as in *o*h dear

factus – 'fac' as in *fa*ctory; 'tus' – this is 'oo' with a mixture of 'u', but not as in r*u*st

est – as in *e*stablish.

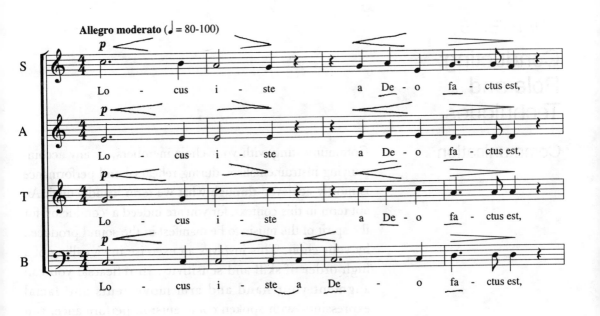

# CHAPTER 5

# Conducting: Role and Techniques

## Communication

Communicating with your choir members, or any accompanying instrumentalists, during rehearsal and performance is mostly achieved through what we term 'conducting'. An apt term in this context, for you are indeed a 'conductor' for the spirit of the music to be manifest in the sound produced by your choir. This involves an exercise in signalling of a high order of skill and sensitivity. In rehearsal you can augment your hand and arm movements and facial expressions with spoken comments; in performance, you will be constrained to silence, unless, as in some small groups or church choirs, you sing or play with them. In this case you have the double responsibility of making music yourself while simultaneously paying attention to the sounds produced by others and you may feel more like a 'leader' than 'conductor'.

Conducting, like all communication, is a two-way process. It demands not only clarity from you in terms of the code you use to give messages to your choir members, but also the capacity to respond to what is going on for them while they are trying to interpret your signals. Of course, much of the ground work for common understanding of the 'language' of conducting for a performance will have been established during rehearsals. You can agree with choir members that when you make certain gestures it is asking for a particular musical response. Some of these gestures and signals will be peculiar to you and your personal style. Some will relate to the special demands of an individual piece of music. Most of the language of conducting, however, has a common base, rooted in musical tradition and in the shared system of gestural communication with which we have all grown up. We would all recognise the finger-to-lips or palm-down spread hands which have signalled 'quiet' from our earliest days, with no need for words. The physical metaphor of body stance and hand, arm and facial movements is a potent part of all communication. Think about how difficult it is to understand an unfamiliar language or accent on the telephone without the aid of vision. Reflect on the importance of the minute aspects of shape of lips and face which enable profoundly deaf people to 'hear'. Some claim that over 80% of 'information' comes from what we see. So in using the silent language of conducting, you have at your finger tips an immensely powerful tool of communication. Like all power tools, it must be handled with care and skill.

## Purpose

The purpose of conducting is to achieve a particular quality of musical expression, by maintaining cohesion, balance and co-ordination, through the responsiveness of a group of singers to your vision of the sound of music. Communication is not only the crux of conducting but also of its outcome, musical expression. David Hill writes:

'Music is a language, and needs to be communicated, and in choral music we have the difficult task of conveying words and their meanings. We have to lift the notes from the page to the hearts and minds of those who are listening. People *must* be moved by listening to music – by the joys, the sadness, the melancholy, the excitement. We, as the experts, will have to some degree failed in our task if these elements are not communicated to the listener. Even if one admires the way in which something is executed, precision, ensemble and tuning do not in themselves make a complete performance.'[1]

The term 'conducting' signifies the important characteristic of *being in touch* with choir members and musicians, engaged in a joint enterprise which, for its success, depends upon give and take on both sides of the podium. You are not only telling people what to do, but also encouraging them to do it cohesively, co-ordinating the individual sounds into a unity. The choir is your instrument, each member a voice with its own particular characteristics. The singers are not only responding to your vision of how the music should be, important though that is, but, through their efforts, they are influencing it, rather as the peculiarities of a violin temper the sound of the music it produces. In 'giving voice', their music will respond to how you have 'given voice' to that vision, enhancing and developing it. It is a continuing process of discovery, as your expertise and musical knowledge is shared with your singers and they, in turn, respond in their interpretation of the music. In this ever-cycling spiral of endeavour, as in all creative acts, the emotional quality of the interchange is important. How you are feeling, how choir members are feeling, the feeling timbre of the music – all are part of the complex interplay involved in conducting. Like all attempts at communication, the logic of the language of conducting may at times be confused, mired by feelings which are hard to express, or remain unacknowledged or unrecognised.

When you feel that you are not getting through to your choir, what do you do? Can you recall the last time that a rehearsal got stuck, or you could not get your message across? Is your choir generally attentive, or do members become restive? Do you get annoyed? Do you think they might be irritated? How often do you check out that your signals are clear to them or that everyone can see?

## Techniques

The size of your choir and the age of its members will influence your approach to conducting. Children may need simpler signals, with more explanation as to meaning. You might ask them to demonstrate how they would signal different moods and speeds; this not only values their side of the communication, gaining attention, but also helps them to get into the feel of the music as well as helping you to clarify your conducting to them. Small groups demand a more intimate and small scale approach, in which little gestures and the hints from facial expression are sufficient to produce a cohesive sound. Large choirs inevitably need more physical space and more expansive movements and exaggerated facial expressions, if everyone is to feel included. Professional singers may need a different approach. Whatever the group size and characteristics of your singers, remember that your approach to conducting them must be geared to their particular needs.

We have said elsewhere that in conducting a choir you can feel isolated and unsupported, an easy target when things go wrong. But don't forget that your choir members, even though they cannot share that leadership responsibility, generally want you to conduct well so that they can sing well together. You all want a successful outcome. Your responsibilities are two-fold – to use your musical expertise to enhance your choir's appreciation of the music and to co-ordinate the sound they produce.

Henry Coward wrote, 'The ever-faithful singers enthusiastically pursued the ideal of their leader.'[2] But, as we have suggested above, this cannot be *blind* pursuit on their part. Your ability to share your vision and to show how it can be achieved is central to the enterprise. Conducting skills and techniques are your valuable tools in this endeavour.

In the metaphor of 'language', which we have been using to think about conducting, structure and grammar are central to understanding and communication. Certain gestures and movements of hands and arms can be regarded as key aspects of the syntax of conducting. Once these are mastered, subtleties of expression can be added.

## Use of the body

Generally, the two hands are the chief 'voices' of the conductor, each playing a vital, but different, role. In the interests of clarity and potential range of expression, they should not, normally, mirror, but complement, each other. The right hand is the time keeper, beating the rhythm with unfailing clarity. The left hand expresses the mood and flow of the music. The face adds a further dimension, communicating through the eyes particularly. The stance of the conductor is also an important indicator; shoulders should be as square-on as possible and relaxed, with feet firmly planted and slightly apart. It may help to imagine yourself to be rooted like a tree, firmly grounded so that your 'branches' can move easily without fear of falling or becoming strained. It is usually clearer to singers if your gestures are largely contained in the space between elbow and hand. Wildly expansive arm movements might fit the mood of the music, but confuse the singers.

## The patterns of beating time

Conducting holds the pulse and beat of the music, demonstrating this to the singers. It also indicates entrances and cessation of the flow of sound, as well as the changes of mood. This is not, necessarily, a metronomically precise activity, as the expression of the sound in the music must also follow its own intrinsic rhythm. Conducting must find a way of bridging these aspects, helping choirs to achieve an overall rhythmic integrity, while maintaining flexibility of expression. There is, in every piece, a hierarchy of rhythm, which gives due weight to particular notes and phrases. The conductor must be able, through gesture, to indicate this to the choir.

Singing 'on the beat' happens via the communication between conductor and singers, when the latter, through practice, acquire an 'inner metronome' for particular pieces. Any rhythmical problem can easily become the focus of an exercise, by breaking down a bar, clapping the rhythm, then singing it. This helps to make singers aware of the subdivisions of the beat and sensitive to its quaver movement and speed. The most notorious rhythm to grasp and perform is the dotted note followed by a half note or tied note equivalent, as you may well appreciate from your own experience. Rhythm is perhaps one aspect of choral singing most difficult to achieve and, paradoxically, most neglected by conductors in choir training.

## Conducting choir and instrumentalists

Clarity in conducting is a vital part of attaining rhythmic and musical integrity. It is further complicated, when your task is to conduct both choir and orchestra or small group of instrumentalists. But, if this an unfamiliar experience, do not be fazed by it. Although there are more musicians with whom to communicate, and the sounds produced by an orchestra are more diverse than that of a choir, the clarity of your beat and gestures will ensure an even flow of music. Remember that you are a catalyst in fitting together the sound of voices and instruments, and that the singers, because generally farther away from you, may well need extra reassurance across the span, both physical and musical, of the orchestra, so do not neglect them. To achieve both choir and orchestra making music together on the beat demands particularly focused attention from you. In this respect, your preparatory gestures are significant, indicating your intention. It is especially important that you have reached an agreement with instrumentalists and singers on the measure of the beat and how you will show it. It is helpful to rehearse, as far as possible, at the speed of the performance, to fix this firmly in people's minds.

The huge potential power of combined choir and orchestra should not lead you to feel overwhelmed. It is your task to control this power, not to be overtaken emotionally by it. Exciting music demands discipline as well as feeling. Accelerandi are especially susceptible to loss of control, or to choir and orchestra having differing views about speed. You must be totally attentive to such hazards, offering musical interpretation through the pacing and weight of phrases, not wallowing in the sounds produced.

All this suggests serious preparation of the score before rehearsal, which is time-consuming but productive. Knowledge of the instruments you will be conducting is advisable, particularly their pitches and transpositions. Mark all leads very clearly, adopting an easy to follow colour coding throughout the score. This system allows you to see in advance what is coming and which leads need your special attention. It is unlikely that you will be able to offer leads to all players and the choir, but you can easily determine which are the instrumental ones most essential to the beat. Try to keep attention on both orchestra and choir, being aware of the more acute problems as they occur. If you are sure of the leaders of the different sections of the orchestra, and have a good communication with them, this will prove invaluable. A simple glance in their direction is often enough to indicate what is required.

Obviously, the clarity of your gestures and glances is even more significant, when conducting choir and orchestra together. We have suggested earlier that gestures and arm movements should be well-moderated, but with a large choir and orchestra the sheer numbers involved and distance between you and them demand larger movements of the body. Your arms should perform as in a semi-circle, being equally visible to singers and instrumentalists. The orchestra, if closer, may need slightly scaled-down gestures, but remember also that your gestures will be affected by the mood of the music.

We would like to suggest that these aspects of conducting should be developed during several joint rehearsals with choir, orchestra and any soloists. The reality is more likely to be that you have one joint practice. In this case, prior separate rehearsals should include briefing about the contribution of the choir or orchestra. A full piano score played during choir rehearsals can help singers to understand their part in the complete work. Listening to recordings can also be useful, so long as they are aware of when other interpretations may differ from your own.

In joint rehearsals, it is advisable not to get bogged down in detail. If this is the final rehearsal, it is essential to go through as much of the work as possible, with a few minutes at the end of each section to note or comment on specific aspects. If things do not go well it is even more important to try to get to the end of the piece, otherwise musicians' confidence can be severely dented. If there is insufficient time to rehearse the music fully, concentrate on the most difficult sections, explaining that you are confident about the rest. Instrumentalists, particularly, seem to appreciate this approach as an efficient use of time. However nervous you may feel about the likely outcome, it is wise to disguise such feelings from your musicians. Performances do sometimes have a surprising way of coming together 'on the night', so long as there has been sufficient earlier preparation.

## Conducting language

We have emphasised the clarity of your conducting language which, while it is your own, is also subject to certain agreed musical conventions. The following drawings and diagrams, which illustrate David Hill's approach, are meant as an aid to reflect on your own skills in this area of music-making. You, as in developing in any language, need to find your own 'voice' and mode of expression in conducting. Practise in front of a mirror, so that you have some idea of how you appear to your singers. If you conduct instrumentalists as well, you may have found that they prefer a different signal from singers, as we have suggested in example 3 on beating in 5. We have included only the most common beats, recognising that the more uncommon ones, such as 7, need to be shown in combinations of the basic patterns, depending on the intrinsic rhythm of the music.

The drawings are shown from the perspective of the choir or orchestra; the diagrams are from that of the conductor.

# Beating patterns

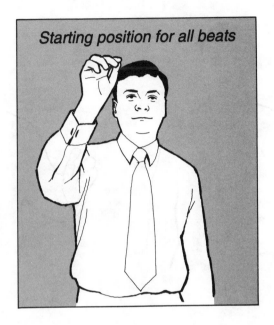

## 2/4 and 6/8 (fast)

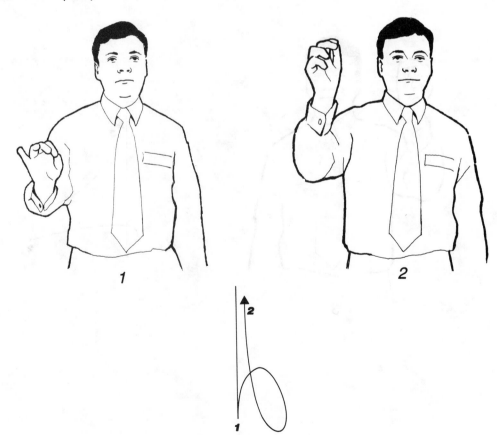

*3/2, 9/8 and 9/4*

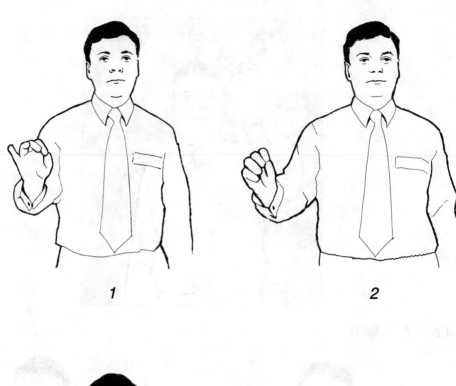

1

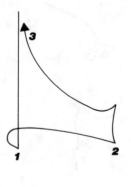

2

3

*6/8 (slow)*

## 4/4, 4/2 and 12/8

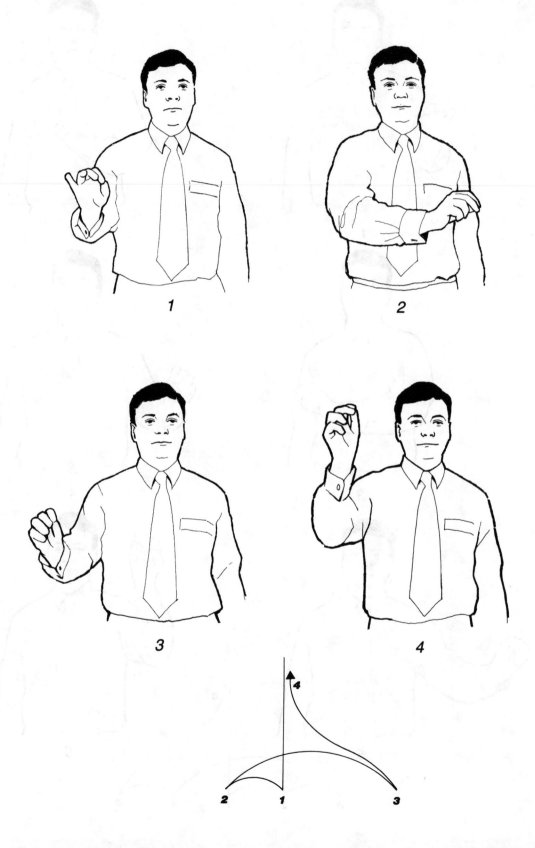

*5/4, 5/8 and 5/2*

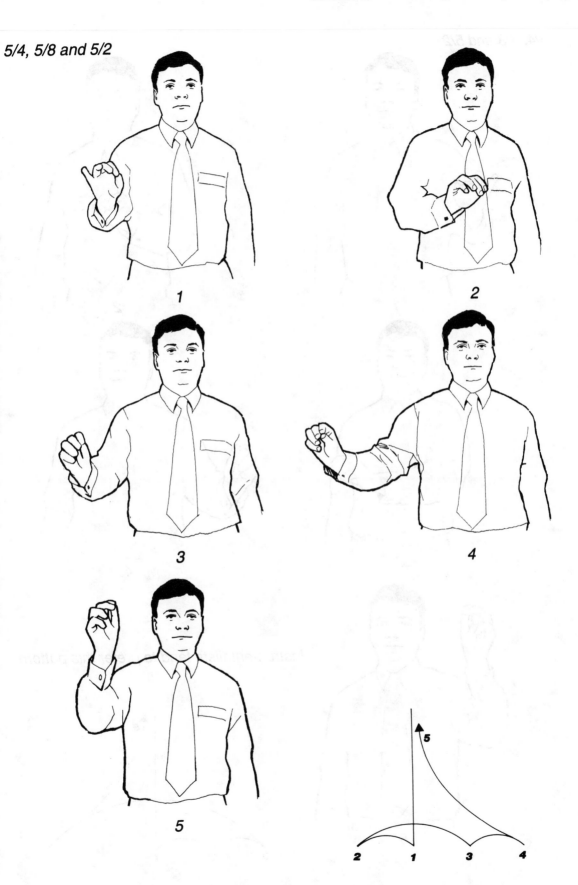

## 5/4, 5/8 and 5/2

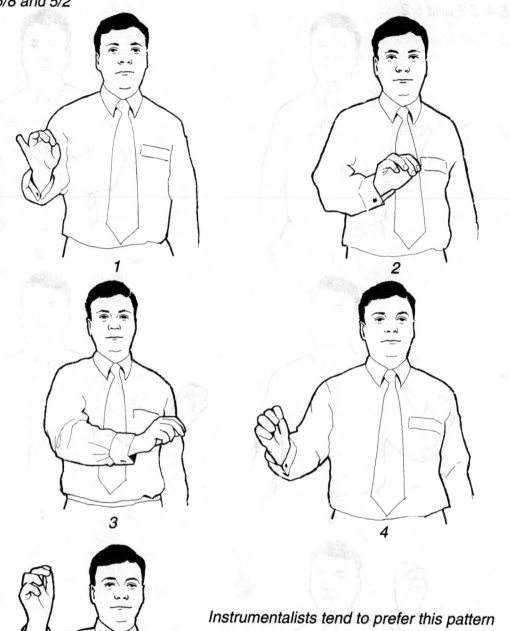

1

2

3

4

5

*Instrumentalists tend to prefer this pattern*

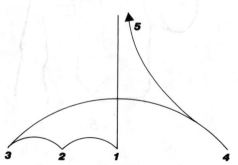

# CHAPTER 6
# The Rehearsal

In this chapter we come to the nub of choir training. We assume that you have made the appropriate plans and preparations for rehearsals to go ahead as scheduled. We explore the purposes and processes of rehearsal, and then in the following chapters suggest some approaches you might find useful.

## The purpose of rehearsal

The rehearsal is the place where 'practice makes perfect', or as close to perfection as it is possible to expect your choir's and your own abilities to achieve. Henry Coward wrote that in seeking this ideal it was most important to pay attention to 'the supreme factor in musical achievement – the rehearsal.' He continued:

'There is a hoary fiction that a final bad rehearsal ensures a good performance. It may be granted that a poor final effort may have its value by making the performers careful at the concert, but it is a mistake to think that a poor or bad rehearsal is anything but a calamity to a society of amateurs. Artistic ideality soon droops in the chilly atmosphere of incompetent dullness; shrivels up in the air of strenuous misdirection of effort; withers and expires in the sultry blasts of querulous irritability.'[1]

Before those of you who work with church choirs protest at the idea of 'performance' being irrelevant to your goal in choir training, we should make it clear that we see liturgical singing as 'performance' of a different sort. David Hill writes:

'There can be no doubt of the importance of the music within the liturgy as an aid to prayer . . . I mention it as a reminder of the enormous responsibility we have, as choir trainers, to bring people closer to God through the music we sing and play. How many times have choirs been criticised for treating the worship as a concert? – and for failing to communicate the message of the music, let alone stirring the emotions of those listening. There is no question in my mind that singing and playing music in church is as much a 'performance' as a soprano singing Lieder or a string quartet playing Beethoven. The chief difference is that the choir in church is relating not just to the congregation (the lieder singer is relating only to her audience), but that the performance (and I use the word advisedly) is taking place in God's house. All that we can do, say, think, or feel relates to Him. "Nothing is too good for God", I once heard Cardinal Hume say. Surely this means that whatever we do must be done to the best of our ability, at whatever level that may be.'[2]

It is well to remember, also, that choral singing today is descended from the ancient Greek and Roman theatrical 'performances', which were essentially religious in character.

Additionally, the rehearsal is the place which offers those enthusiastic to sing the opportunity to do so regularly. Not only the quality of the final performance motivates them, but also the enjoyment of singing together frequently in the rehearsals. Nothing is more corrosive of such enjoyment, and therefore of singers' commitment, than rehearsals which feel as though they have been a waste of time and energy. This emphasis may be rather different from your own, which may be geared more specifically to using the rehearsal to perfect the outcome, ie 'performance', rather than seeing it as an end in itself. The rehearsal, therefore, has to satisfy both singers and conductor if that elusive but essential quality, 'motivation', is to be sustained.

This suggests the necessity, sometimes, for a compromise in the rehearsal's content and process, between what the choir and the conductor want. Its careful and sensitive management is about getting as much good work done as possible within a limited time. In order to achieve this, your understanding of the strengths and weaknesses of your choir is paramount in both planning and running rehearsals. How you manage the cycles of energy and effort which are inevitably part of group endeavour; how you pace your expectations of your singers during a particular rehearsal and over a series; how you introduce exercises to 'warm-up' the voice, extend its range, increase its variation in colour and mood; how you respond to difficulties – all of these (and more) govern what you and the singers get from a rehearsal.

Before we explore this territory further, we suggest you ask yourself:

---

When I begin a rehearsal, how do I start my interaction with choir members?– and how have I prepared for what we are about to do? What do I know about my choir? Are they amateur, coming from a variety of jobs to sing after a hard day's work, and therefore tired? Are they music professionals, meeting to sing with me during the course of a normal day? Are they familiar with each other? What is their level of skill in singing together or individually? What are my expectations of them? Do I know what their expectations are of me? When I begin a rehearsal, how do I get the music and the singing started? (You will find further questions suggesting themselves according to your own particular circumstances as director.)

---

As we have already suggested, the first several minutes of your interaction with the choir will set the tone for the remainder of the rehearsal and will determine whether or not it is productive and enjoyable. We have discussed the importance of the relationship between you and choir members in an earlier chapter and here make recommendations about approaches to managing that relationship within the context of the rehearsal.

## Rehearsal methods

Henry Coward suggested that there were three main approaches taken by choir directors, each with its good and bad points, and each appropriate at different stages of preparing a particular piece of music.[3] He emphasised, however, that, whatever the approach adopted *it was foolish to expect a choir to give full musical and textual expression until both notes and words were well-known.* In other words, the appropriate timing of a conductor's expectations and demands upon a choir was crucial to success in rehearsal. After all, rehearsing is about learning, and we would not expect to be fluent in a foreign language after two lessons. This means that the *learning points* of each rehearsal should be carefully anticipated and prepared for by you, with the appropriate exercises. Finding the appropriate methods to best achieve this is not always easy; choirs may surprise in their ready capacity to grasp some points and dismally disappoint in others. Flexibility is, therefore, the key.

You might recognise yourself in one or more of the three following, somewhat caricatured, methods which Henry Coward describes as 'The Conventional Generalising; The Critical (or hypercritical) Particularizing; and The Compartmental Specializing'.

• The conventional and generalised approach

This is probably the most common method, used by the majority of choir trainers. It consists of repeatedly going through the music in full, until its general outline is taken on board by the singers. It has virtue in that it is generally the only way to acquaint a choir with a particular piece of music. Its limitations lie in the lack of attention to detail, and the possibility of boring the singers and deadening the resulting sound if it is used exclusively. It needs to be augmented by other approaches.

• The critical/particular approach

This is characterised by seeking perfection in each detail of the piece. It is necessary at certain stages of rehearsal, when the singers are familiar with the music and text, though, as we have previously said, 'perfection' is a chimera. It is totally counter-productive in the early stages of learning a piece, when it may mean that too much stopping and starting, because of mistakes, leads to the music never being sung as a whole. Continually focusing on one or two of the parts, while the rest of the choir waits expectantly, can lead to tension and irritation as well as anxiety – none of which are conducive to either learning or singing.

• The 'compartmental specializing' approach

Henry Coward suggests that this is little known or practised, yet it is likely that many of you will recognise it as an approach you do adopt from time to time. It consists of focusing all attention on some special topic or aspect of the music, to the neglect of everything else. Sometimes, when trying to get a choir to achieve a particular sound in a particular phrase, it is easy to get hooked into losing perspective on the whole and failing to recognise the mounting concern and agitation of the singers that other aspects which they have been practising are ignored. This is not to deny the value of this approach at some times, particularly when the music is receiving its final polish prior to performance. Henry Coward made a list of likely features demanding 'specialization', to which you can no doubt add. He wrote:

'Amongst the many features that call for specialization we may include the working up to a climax; the polishing of a *pianissimo* phrase; the obtaining of a perfect attack; the management of the *crescendo* and the *diminuendo;* the realising of the dynamic and emotional *sforzandos* and pressure notes; the clarifying – to the listener – of close imitations; the development of marked entrances; the perfecting of vowels and consonants; the marking of breathing places; the unifying of tone-quality; and the developing of characteristic tonal effects . . .'[4]

Each approach has its uses; each rehearsal may need a combination of these approaches, the balance of which depends upon the stage of the learning of any particular piece. As a general rule, the conventional and generalised method should be used in all early rehearsals of a new piece, thus giving the singers the opportunity to get into the spirit as well as the notes of the music and to hear it as a whole.

Concentrating on special effects or difficulties should begin *in small doses at first* so as not to dishearten the singers, as soon as you sense that they are ready to absorb the required detail; it can offer a breather to spend a few moments giving an example yourself (on piano or, better still, in voice) of the phrase in question, before asking the singers to try for it. It may mean introducing some special exercises to increase vocal technique; these may also be regarded as useful punctuations in changing the pace of, and thus energising, the rehearsal. It is wise to take account of the places where you might want to ask only some of the choir to work, for instance, where there are renowned difficulties for one of the parts, so that the remainder of the singers do not lose attention. Sometimes it can be helpful to ask everyone to sing the difficult part until it is mastered, before returning to their own 'voice'. By the time of the final one or two rehearsals, the choir should be ready for larger doses of this approach, to put the final touches to a, by then, well-known piece and make it ready for performance.

At this stage the critical/particular approach may also be advantageous, as the singers will be relaxed in their understanding of the music and their ability to express it well. Henry Coward commented:

'The conductor will find that the worry to himself and the fretting to the choir have now disappeared, because the singers, being in a state of preparedness, can give full attention and practical effect to any new demand of interpretation. Further, at this stage they become by their responsiveness fellow helpers, almost anticipating every wish; and furthermore, they enjoy the polishing process when they feel that they can realise the conductor's ideas. There is now no irritation at being stopped again and again; in fact they like it, because they feel every interruption means improvement in one point or another, and this makes them feel the joy of successful conquest, and they leave the rehearsal room shaking hands with themselves at what has been attempted and accomplished. As to the conductor, he will go home delighted, and refreshed in spirit though perhaps tired in body. For has he not had the joy of seeing – or rather hearing – his ideals of beauty materialise? Like another Aladdin, he has only to call, and lo! an artistic edifice has sprung to life at his bidding – happy man!'[5]

or 'woman!' we would add.

From such rousing poetry, which we hope resonates with your own experience of the successful culmination of rehearsals, we move into more practical matters to do with what we have termed 'warming-up'.

# CHAPTER 7
# Warming-up

In this chapter we include general discussion of the purposes of warming-up to be followed in chapter 8 by specific exercises which you might find useful with your choir. As we have frequently mentioned, *learning* is central to successful choral work – learning the music and words; learning to sing together; learning to produce a good sound overall; learning to produce the voice individually. All learning activity, to which singing is no exception, depends upon concentration, repetition and practice, and the permission to 'get it wrong'; the context of the learning and the attitude and skill of the teacher or coach can hinder or help. Since singing is very intensely involved with the expression of self, the possibilities for feeling anxious or tense are legion; too much anxiety spells death to confidence and, therefore, to the sort of relaxed concentration needed to 'give voice' fully. Warming-up is an essential precursor to effective learning, because it sets the tone as well as the scene, clarifies expectations and needs, enables people to feel relaxed and hopeful that they will do well. In choral singing, warming-up has social, physical and psychological components, which interrelate to influence the musical outcome.

## Warming-up socially

The social atmosphere of rehearsal can help or hinder its success. If people feel uncomfortable with each other they are likely to be inhibited in their singing. Making sure that the atmosphere is congenial, that attention is given to the socialising aspects of being in the choir, may not be as important for you personally as it is for your singers. But you neglect it at the risk of losing the motivation of some singers and creating a heavy, and therefore, musically deadening, context of work together. The old adages 'all work and no play' and 'those that play together, stay together' offer useful folk wisdom to the choir director. This means allowing time during the rehearsals for people to talk to each other; recognising when some event, either personal or to do with the community, is significant for the choir; starting your rehearsals with your own social graces to the fore.

## Warming-up physically

In the chapter on The Voice, we described the physiology of singing and emphasised the fact that the voice is the instrument of the whole body, not simply of the vocal chords. If the body is to use its instrument effectively, it must achieve both relaxation and concentration, so that the energy of the breath is free to resonate the vibrations of the vocal chords through the cavities which are the soundboards of the voice. Relaxation and concentration are not in opposition, but work together to produce the sort of open-throated sound aspired to by most choirs. Both physical and psychological components are involved interdependently in achieving this. Some 'social' influences, to which we have referred earlier also apply. Here we concentrate on some of the physical aspects which can inhibit or enhance the sound of the voice.

Choir members, (and directors), may arrive for rehearsal tired and stressed, for a variety of reasons – after a day's work, because of examinations, trying to fit the rehearsal into a busy schedule. You can doubtless think of many more. It is helpful to take time at the beginning of the session to do one or two simple stretching or moving or relaxing or breathing exercises, particularly involving the upper torso and preferably standing up. These can be combined with some aspect of social warm-up, so that two people are working together. Singers often need to be reminded of the importance of correct posture for singing, whether standing or sitting. Suggestions and exercises are outlined later for you to try out or amend.

## Warming-up psychologically

It is, in a sense, misleading, to separate out these different aspects of warm-up, but we hope that this will enable you to reflect upon which components you most need to attend to in relation to your own choir and your own skills. We have already stressed the importance of your attitude in influencing how your choir gives voice and how your initial contact at each rehearsal sets the scene for the work together.

The psychology of singing has been referred to earlier (see Chapter 2) and not only involves confidence and concentration, but also the ability to enter into the nature of the music being sung – entering the soul of the music.

This is not always easy for many people and exercises which set the imagination of your choir going into a better rapport with the music and a better understanding of how they can produce their voices will reap dividends in musical sound. They need to use this faculty when trying to visualise or otherwise appreciate how their bodies and minds work to produce song; how to get into how it feels when the voice is produced openly and freely; to recognise and reproduce the buzz of clear resonance and focus. We offer some specific ideas to develop the imaginative capacity of your choir in general in relation to the music you are performing and the aspects of voice production you want to develop. We repeat our earlier exhortations that you should be both flexible and sensitive in encouraging this, as to use imagination in singing, to 'give voice' openly means that sometimes the singers will get it wrong.

## Warming-up the voice

This is the aspect of warming-up which most choir directors acknowledge as important, though it is not invariably part of every rehearsal.

---

Take time to reflect on whether you always find time for this, and if so how? Perhaps there are occasions when time is pressing, there is much to get through and voice exercises take a back seat.

---

On the other hand, for some choirs, there is a weary sameness about voice warm-ups. One can almost hear the groan as the same old exercises get wheeled out again, for the sake of satisfying the letter, though not the spirit, of the principles involved – 'warm-ups for the voice are a good thing, therefore they shall be done!'

We suggest that there are two aspects to voice warm-ups: getting the instrument itself into flexible and responsive mode with regard to specific techniques; and facilitating the singers' tackling of specific pieces of music. We emphasise that in both senses *warming-up is not simply a beginning of rehearsal activity*. While some aspects of getting the voice started and responsive are more obviously useful at the beginning of a rehearsal and involve generalities to do with breathing, focus, resonance etc, warm-ups should always be related to what is going to be asked of the voice at any particular time by specific pieces of music, and therefore might take place at different points throughout the rehearsal.

One of the considerations which will affect the punctuation of the rehearsal with vocal warm-ups is the recognition of a choir's attention-span. This will vary with the age and experience of the choir, amongst other things (including the physical surroundings and level of comfort). Most choirs will be more attentive at the beginning of a rehearsal, and lose mindfulness and energy as the practice continues. Voice warm-ups can be useful wake-up points, grabbing attention again as well as moving the choir into another mood of music or reminding them of some of the basics. It is generally recognised that the attention span of an average audience is between 10 and 15 minutes. Choir members, by the nature of their engagement in the process, are likely to remain attentive for longer, but it is advisable not to overestimate this. Warm-ups can also introduce a change of pace into rehearsals, perhaps lightening mood and relaxing the intensity of focus on a particular piece.

The exercises for this aspect of warming-up refer back to the earlier discussion on voice production and cover what we consider, in relation to the individual voice, to be the basics of support, breath control, resonance and focus, intonation and the development of the variety of line and colour demanded by specific pieces of music. Another important 'basic' is the cohesion and musicality of the choir in ensemble, and the exercises include this factor also.

You may have your own favourites to add to these suggestions, or wish to combine them to cover more than one aspect of warming-up.

Your ability to share your vision of the choir's sound is important. Warming-up is a singers-focused activity, encouraging the best from the joining of the individual voices in the choir. Your example of singing or doing what is required in the exercises, offering a 'model', is invaluable. Making sure that choir members understand the purpose of the exercises, without getting too bogged down in technical detail about how the voice is produced, will encourage them further.

Whatever your choice of vocal warm-up exercises it is important to remember that, particularly initially, *they should always be done within the comfortable range of the singers.* This is especially so for children's voices, which are much more vulnerable to the effects of repeated strain or misuse. There will be times when your aim is to extend the singers' range, but exercises to achieve this should be kept to times when the voices are in form and going well. Rather like a car, which we would not expect to start and immediately drive at 70 mph if we want to preserve the engine, the voices of your choir need equal consideration.

## Warming-up for performance

There is often little time to prepare for performance, except in a final rehearsal which may have taken place hours or days previously, and not necessarily in the actual performance venue. Given all that we have written about the importance of warming-up the voice, it would be invaluable to offer choirs the opportunity to do so immediately before performing. Environmental and time constraints often millitate against this, however. It is, therefore, wise to bear this in mind and to suggest ways in which singers can do their own warm-ups, to relax and focus, before a performance, particularly in relation to the physical and psychological aspects of preparation. Singers should be encouraged to arrive in good time, to be familiar with the surroundings, and to think about posture and voice production for some minutes beforehand. Your presence and reminders can be both a support and encouragement at such times. It may be helpful for you to have a priority shortlist of items you would like the choir to concentrate on in relation to a particular piece as an aide memoire at a final rehearsal. No new exercises should be introduced immediately before a performance, and some of the exercises, particularly the physical ones, we suggest can be practised individually and relatively soundlessly by choir members.

It is also worth remembering that, if the final rehearsal takes place only hours before the performance, that the best should be saved for the latter. Pushing a choir to do its utmost, in terms of range of tone and expression, at the final rehearsal, can lead to fatigue and flatness in the performance. Tired people produce tired and tense voices.

To conclude this general section on 'warming-up', we emphasise that the nature, age and particular voices of the choir must claim the utmost attention. As we have noted in the chapter on voice production, your approach to and expectations of children will be different from what you require of adults; your work with amateurs will demand different attitudes from your work with professionals; the different motivations and purposes of the choir and its members will determine its response to you.

# CHAPTER 8
# Warming-up Exercises

In this, and the following chapter, we offer suggestions and exercises gleaned from practical experience. We put forward a variety of activities, designed to achieve specific results. We do not envisage that you will find it necessary to try all of them, but that you will select according to your choir's needs. Most importantly, we urge you to try out the exercises before using them so that you can be quite sure why you are selecting or adapting them and can check out whether they work for you.

As we have repeated throughout this book, all aspects of singing are connected, but it is often useful to 'trouble-shoot', when problems arise, by analysing which specific area needs attention. We limit 'physical' aspects in this chapter to posture and relaxation, while recognising that all singing is 'physical'. We assume that breathing is so central to voice production and training that we include it in the next chapter on warming up and exercising the singing voice.

## The social context

The following suggestions aim to increase the sense of cohesion within a choir, contributing to the confidence, relaxation and enjoyment of the singers and to their motivation to produce the best in their singing. Your prompt arrival at rehearsals will always be appreciated and make the choir members feel valued for their contribution to the joint effort. A sense of humour is also an invaluable asset, provided that it is not exercised at their expense.

We assume that you will have already prepared a plan for any particular rehearsal.

Are choir members aware of which music they will be tackling? Have you asked them to do some work on particular pieces?

Sometimes a spontaneous response to the circumstances of a particular rehearsal is called for and may mean adjusting part of your careful preparations. The balance between achieving your goal and being aware of your singers' needs is often a fine one. We cannot emphasise enough that choral singing is a group activity and, as such, depends upon human relations and interaction for its energy.

## Greetings

**Time**

A few minutes (depending upon how well choir members already know each other).

**Purpose**

To engage with the choir; to help singers engage with each other.

**Posture**

Sitting comfortably.

**Activities**

1   Greet the choir appropriately – 'Good evening/morning etc'. Ask how they are feeling? Make any relevant comment about the context of the rehearsal – weather, are they too hot/cold etc? Physical environment – are they too cramped? Can everyone see/hear etc?
    Welcome any new members.

2   Ask singers to turn to a neighbour. Do they know each other's names? If not, introduce themselves.
    Ask them (in pairs) to ask each other how they are and reply.
    Ask them to tell each other (in pairs) one good or amusing thing that happened to them that day.
    Ask them to tell each other what they feel about the music they are about to sing.

---

Think of other questions relevant to the particular circumstances/characteristics of the choir that would be good social warm-ups.

---

3   Ask them to move to sit next to someone from a different 'voice', preferably someone not known to them. Let them introduce themselves, then say what they like about singing in the choir; or what might be difficult for their particular part in the music being rehearsed; or what they like/dislike about being a soprano, alto, bass, tenor. *Think of other relevant questions.*

4　Ask them to remain in 'mixed voices' for the next activities. An element of surprise, though not of shock, can help to enliven each rehearsal.

## The physical aspects

Choir members should know enough about how the voice is produced for the following activities to make sense to them (see chapter on voice production). Remind them that the voice is the instrument of the whole body. Explain the importance of a free flow of breath, the energy and support of the voice, in producing a clear and focused sound. Identify the body's resonating cavities, and the main muscles used in breath control. Emphasise the importance of relaxation and posture, either sitting or standing, in achieving a resonant and focused sound. Make sure that the choir knows about the work of other muscles, face and tongue for example, in producing voice.

Be sure to give sufficient explanation, but not too much, and not all at once! Some of it will be internalised and become second nature as you remind the choir at each rehearsal of why they are being asked to do particular exercises or activities. You might want to concentrate only on particular aspects at given rehearsals, or ask members to practise some things on their own. A simple handout can assist singers to understand why such exercises are helpful.

We have categorised the following activities, but suggest that you choose as suits you and your choir. Everything is connected in singing, in any case, and it might be useful to move from what we have described as a 'physical' exercise, to a vocal one and back to achieve a particular result.

---

Experiment, invent your own activities. Ask your choir to tell you what works for them.

---

Some choirs may feel somewhat inhibited at first, but learning to be at ease with each other will be a valuable asset in singing well together.

*Relaxation – awareness of body and muscles*

**Time**

A few minutes, depending on how mixed with other activities.

**Purpose**

To develop a relaxed stance; to increase awareness of body and muscle control.

**Activities**

In the same places in which they ended the 'greetings' activities if in 'mixed voices', or ask the choir to mix themselves, ask singers to stand and do one or more of the following. Demonstrate what you mean.

1   Stretch and yawn as if getting out of bed in the morning. Be aware of what is happening to your breathing and the action of the diaphragm as you do it. Be aware of the sound and sensation of yawning and what is happening to the tongue and soft palate.

2   Roll shoulders as if you have been sitting too long at the theatre/cinema and feel stiff. Roll shoulders forward a few times, then backwards, together and separately. Be aware of what is happening to the bony structure around the upper torso and to the musculature of the back. Finish with both hands hanging loosely by the sides.

3   With sufficient space, perhaps turning sideways-on if this is cramped, raise arms slowly to a count of 'up – two – three,' then down to a count of 'down – two – three' several times. Be aware of what is happening to the rib cage, diaphragm and breathing. Suggest inhaling to the 'up' counts, exhaling to the 'down' counts. Repeat several times.

4   Standing with feet parallel, weight evenly balanced, head slightly and loosely bowed from the neck looking at the feet, breathe slowly from the toes upward, raising the head to look forward as the breath 'travels' up the body. Breathe out reversing the movements. Be aware of the rooted feeling that grows in the feet and legs and lower body, the relaxation that occurs in the upper torso and head.

5   Grimace silently to each other in pairs (sitting or standing), looking at each other with as many different

expressions and as much exaggerated facial movement as possible. Go from smiles to anger to sadness; make each other laugh. Be aware of the stretching and pulling of the facial muscles and what is happening to the tongue.

6 In pairs, standing, ask each person in turn to relax first one, then the other arm, so that the partner can lift it and let it flop down again. Each person gives feedback on the weight and floppiness of the arm to the partner. Be aware of what is happening to the upper torso as the arm is raised and lowered.

7 Reduce tension in the upper back by working in pairs, each in turn placing a hand, palm outward, between the shoulder blades of the other. The hand should rest gently but firmly. The recipient breathes comfortably but slowly; both think 'calm'. Reverse roles after a few breaths.

## Posture and support

Some of the above exercises influence posture (see also p 22). In addition, asking the singers to imagine a stream of energy rising up from the ground, through their toes and the rest of their bodies, will give the sensation of openness of flow through the resonating cavities and help them to experience feeling 'grounded'. They might find feeling like a tree, firmly rooted yet free at the top to sway in the wind, a helpful image. Ask them to wiggle their knees, when standing to test their balance and groundedness. Whether standing or sitting, singers should feel evenly balanced, with a straight back and expectant stance to the head.

Most rehearsals are spent for the majority of time sitting, while performances invariably are given standing. Sitting well, therefore, is an invaluable aid to singing well. So often choirs rehearse in inadequate surroundings. Make sure that, whatever the space and size of chairs available, singers know how to sit well. Only the front of the chair should be used, with both feet planted squarely and firmly, taking the body weight evenly between them. The back should be straight, the abdomen free, so that abdominal muscles and diaphragm can work effectively.

**Activity**

Ask singers to sit feeling relaxed and rooted, as described above and to take a long deep breath to your counting. Then ask them to sit back in their chairs, curving the spine and crumpling the midrift, slumping shoulders forward. Change posture to a more 'military style', with shoulders pushed excessively back. In each posture, ask them to note what is happening to their breathing.

In order to induce a helpful sitting stance, suggest that women have to accommodate a bustle as well as themselves on the chair; that men are sitting on a narrow pub bench; that children, who are less likely to need such assistance, are perched on a narrow wall.

The Alexander technique may be familiar to you. It offers a fund of ideas about posture and the importance for general well-being, as well as for singing, of maintaining a well-aligned body.

# The psychological aspects

Many of the above activities also involve the psychology of singing. In this section, we focus on the importance of the imagination in producing a wide range of vocal expression. Mind and body unite in producing song. Confidence in self-expression is basic to what we want to achieve in choral singing, even if this might seem to imply individualistic unevenness of tone. An individual's ability to vary the range and tone and colouration of 'normal' sound, in speech, underlies the capacity for awareness of such variables in song. The following activities, designed to encourage the sort of 'letting go' that results in relaxed and enjoyable singing, are based not on sung but on spoken sound. Children, especially, often need permission to relax and enjoy their music-making together.

## Exercises

**Purpose**

To explore the capacity for range of vocal expression; to develop confidence in using and projecting the voice.

**Time**

From a few minutes to as long as you feel is necessary at any particular time.

**Activities**

1 Calling 'hello' from various imagined distances. Ask singers to imagine first of all that they are within conversation distance from their listener, then lengthen the imagined gap until they are shouting across the length of a football pitch.

2 Ask singers to imagine that they are running a stall in Petticoat Lane on a busy Sunday. Ask them to call out their wares in competition with each other.

3 Suggest that singers are in a dangerous situation, in which they must whisper clearly to a friend without letting a nearby enemy know of their existence. Give them a phrase, such as – 'Can you hear me?' to repeat as clearly and quietly as possible.

4 Ask singers to pretend that they are dogs: barking greeting; growling dangerously; whining in pain or through danger.

5 Suggest that singers are water creatures, flowing down river. Ask them to imitate the sounds of water flowing – fast, then slowly, then trickling.

6 Ask singers to imagine that they are clocks all ticking to different times, some fast, some slow, some loud, some softly, some with cuckoo calls and some with chimes to mark the passing hours. Give each section a different type of clock. See which 'wins'. Ask singers to be aware of what is happening to their tongues and mouths particularly in the 'tick-tock' noises.

7 Ask singers to imitate the sound of police or ambulance sirens; owls; chickens clucking. Suggest that they note the difference in what is happening to face, tongue and breathing in each case.

8 Ask singers to use a recitative style in turning to a neighbour to ask: 'Are you really there?', the neighbour replying, 'Yes, I'm really here.' Repeat in as many moods as you have time for.

# CHAPTER 9

# Voice Production and Projection Exercises

## Warm-ups and ideas

We dedicate a whole chapter to this aspect of singing, recognising its central importance in producing the sort of sound to which you and your choir aspire. We make an assumption that you are aiming for a 'forward' or 'open-throated' sound, whether working with children or adults. As David Hill states:

'To say that English choirs have a particular way of singing which has nothing to do with solo singers is really irrelevant. All singing is about the production of the voice. We have to get away from the idea that what we think is right, and do more serious study of the subject; a more European outlook on vocal training is probably to be encouraged.'[1]

We have mentioned earlier the value of thinking of the voice as circular, with the sinus areas as central to good resonance. Henry Coward wrote in similar vein about what he termed 'nasal resonance' (which is not synonymous with singing through the nose):

'By "singing with nasal resonance" is meant the enriching of the voice by so adjusting the sounding air current that part of the "tube of air" which passes over the vocal chords, goes behind the uvula and passes into the nasal cavities, there producing sympathetic overtones which blend with and enrich the sound which proceeds, in the main, from the mouth.'[2]

As we suggested earlier vocal warm-ups are useful *not only at the beginning of a rehearsal, but at points all the way through,* in relation to the particular pieces being practised. They can help singers to focus attention on different aspects of voice production, as well as introduce a new mood or style, and they can act as attention-holders through a long and concentrated session. It is important for you to be able to demonstrate what you want the choir to do each time and that they should understand why. Equally, the voices should not be pushed, either in range or volume, especially at the beginning. *It is usually advisable to start with downward phrases in the middle voice.*

If your natural voice is very different from those in the choir, as often happens when working with children, it is useful to have a 'model' with similar vocal characteristics to illustrate the exercises.

Voice-developing exercises should generally be short and relevant to the effect you are aiming for; easily memorised, so that attention can be given fully to the activity rather than diverted to remembering; and effective in convincing your singers that they can achieve the desired sound. At times, when helping the choir to deal with a particularly difficult passage, you might find it necessary to prolong a particular voice development exercise. So long as the singers understand why and you and they feel that the exercise is achieving the desired effect, this should not be a problem. It is wise to stop such an activity when it is clear that it is not working or when voices and singers are tired.

Don't forget to stop and tell your singers when they are doing well in addition to pointing out the need to concentrate on particular exercises to improve the quality of their singing.

An example of a general warm-up in mid-voice:

| *legato* | | | | |
|---|---|---|---|---|
| mah | mah | mah | mah | mah |
| can | you | come | to | tea? |
| cah | cah | cah | cah | cah |
| so | who | knows | you | too? |

NB The cue size notes indicate the range within which it is appropriate that the exercises should be done.

## Breathing

We remind you that the muscles of breath control should not be solely associated with the diaphragm. Over-emphasis on diaphragm can hinder rather than assist useful breath control for singing. Emphasis should be on breathing *as naturally and quietly as possible.* It is not necessary, and may be counterproductive, to tell your singers to breathe before entrances, though it can be helpful to suggest breathing places in sustained phrases. Raising awareness about the importance of support from all the abdominal muscles, not exclusively the diaphragm, in 'intercostal' breathing (see illustrations p.23) is the significant aspect of the following exercises. Learning the supportive 'tuck' of the abdomen, which controls the flow and energy of the breath, is of great value to singers in good voice production.

### Exercises

**Purpose**

To raise awareness of the function of the abdominal muscles in inter-costal breathing; to develop control of these muscles.

**Time**

A few minutes, possibly combined with other exercises.

**Activities**

1 Ask choir members to imagine that there is a burning candle at the end of each finger. They must try to blow it out with a 'pht! pht!' sound on each finger. Ask them to be aware of what is happening to the abdominal muscles, including the diaphragm, as they do this.

2 Look at the illustration on page 23 and ask singers to replicate this with their hands, so that the tips of the first two fingers of each hand touch, one hand resting lightly on the mid-front across the diaphragm, the other, with thumb tucked in, resting on the side of the rib cage. Ask them to inhale, and note the fingers parting; to exhale and note the fingers meeting.

3 Ask singers to sit upright and imagine holding against themselves a delicate piece of coral between their hands at the level of their diaphragms. They should breathe to long counts in and out while doing this. Then suggest that they bend forward and do the same and ask what would happen to the delicate coral. (This demonstrates the connection between posture and breathing.)

4   Ask singers to imagine that the lower abdomen is a balloon, being filled by them and then held at the neck until they decide to release it. The breath is taken in through the mouth until the body feels full of air, then you might ask them to hold or release it slowly or quickly, to contrast the different sensations.

5   Ask singers to respond naturally to you after you say 'Hello'; they should realise that in normal everyday speech, we are not aware of diaphragm or breath control – we simply breathe. 'Just breathing' normally is a useful contrast to over-breathing and over-concentration on the diaphragm.

6   Ask singers to make a high pitched yapping sound, like a small dog, and to note the movements of the abdominal muscles as they do so.

**Trouble-shooting**

If voices sound breathy, as a result of over-breathing or poor breath control, the following exercises can be helpful. They should be sung lightly, staccato (to emphasise the 'tuck' of breath control), with clear vowels. Beware of the temptation to sing 'n' before the sounds starting with 'd'.

*Exercise 1*

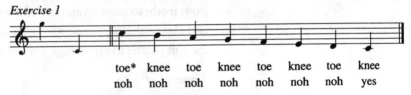

|  |  |  |  |  |  |  |  |
|---|---|---|---|---|---|---|---|
| toe* | knee | toe | knee | toe | knee | toe | knee |
| noh | noh | noh | noh | noh | noh | noh | yes |

* *Don't allow a stray 'w' to creep in on the word 'toe'.*

*Exercise 2*

|  |  |  |  |  |  |  |  |
|---|---|---|---|---|---|---|---|
| dah | dee | dah | dee | dah | dee | dah | dee |

*Exercise 3*

| bee | dee | boo | doo | bee |
|---|---|---|---|---|

*Exercise 4*

| ee____ah | ah | ah | ah | ah____ee |
|---|---|---|---|---|
| tee tee tee toe | toe | toe | toe | toe____tee |

## Open throat and tongue position

We recommend that you review the section on voice production if you are not clear about the advantages of this. In summary, the benefits are greater resonance and focus and avoidance of over-production of the 'head' voice and a characteristic hooty sound.

Although it is generally useful to encourage the mouth to be well-open, with the bottom jaw loose, some singers will find it easier when producing high notes especially to close the mouth slightly, as in a smile. The 'singers' smile' is promoted by many voice coaches as it changes the musculature of the face, opening up resonating cavities. Over-opening creates a tight jaw. So long as your singers are producing the sound you are after, you can afford to be flexible about how they get there. Voice production depends upon individual as well as common characteristics.

The following exercises suggest different ways of achieving a rounded and open sound. Beware, in the sung examples, of pushing voices beyond their comfortable range.

### Exercises

**Purpose**

To encourage correct placing of the tongue behind the lower front teeth; to raise awareness of the difference between open and closed throat; to encourage an open throat and raising of the soft palate; to encourage a relaxed jaw.

**Time**

As long as you think is necessary.

**Activities**

1  Ask singers to place the tongue correctly, then with mouth open, place a finger on it to 'hold it in place' and sing down a simple scale to 'ah'. Then suggest that they deliberately raise the tongue to the roof of the mouth and do the same exercise. Then repeat with the tongue 'held down'. Ask them to note what is happening in the mouth and throat each time and the difference in the feel and the sound.

2  Ask singers to sing, with parted lips, 'hyng' on a descending 5 note scale, changing to 'ah' on the bottom note. Note what is happening to the tongue, soft palate and throat and jaw. Emphasise keeping the jaw loose.

hyng⸻ah

3   Ask singers to allow the lower jaw to fall down, while singing a very slurred glissando octave gently up and down, rather like a lazy fire engine.

4   Ask singers to repeat quickly on the same note 'mah – blah – lah – lah' etc, being aware of what the tongue is doing. Repeat on a descending scale.

mahblahlah   mahblahlah   mahblahlah

mahblahlah   mahblahlah   mahblahlah   mahblahlah   mahblahlah

5   Open the mouth in a gentle yawn, being aware of what is happening to the soft palate.

6   Inhale as in a soft snore, allowing the soft palate to make the characteristic sound, while the jaw loosens.

7   Sing the following exercises quickly to keep the jaw flexible.

*Exercise 1*

yah   yah   yah   yah   yah   yah   yah

*Exercise 2*

yah   yah   yah   yah   yah   yah

yah   yah   yah   yah   yah   yah   yah   yah

## Focus and resonance

The preceeding exercises should assist in the production of a resonant and focused sound, but there are other factors, many of which are rooted in the contribution of the imagination to singing. The singers' perception of what is happening in their bodies when they produce a resonant voice is an important aspect of their learning to re-produce the effect later.

*Exercises*

**Purpose**

To develop a focused sound; to achieve resonance in individual voices; to assist in voice projection.

**Time**

As long as you think necessary at any stage of the rehearsal.

**Activities**

1   Focus: Ask singers to think of gathering the sound in their mouths before projecting it at a particular point across the room. Wall-set plugs or door handles are useful in this respect. Imagining that they are focusing a narrow beam of light or a camera can be useful. With this image in mind, sing quietly a single note, using 'oo-oh-ah', on a descending scale. Then change the vowels, as in the examples which follow. Ask singers to make minimal movements of the external mouth and lips and to be aware of how the shape changes internally.

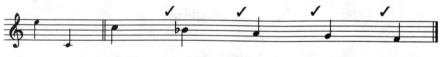

|  |  |  |  |  |
|---|---|---|---|---|
| oo–oh–ah | oo–oh–ah | oo–oh–ah | oo–oh–ah | oo–oh–ah |
| see–red–car | see–red–car | see–red–car | see–red–car | see–red–car |
| see–blue–car | see–blue–car | see–blue–car | see–blue–car | see–blue–car |
| blue–so–far | blue–so–far | blue–so–far | blue–so–far | blue–so–far |

NB If you invent your own exercises, take care not to start on high notes with closed vowels as this can create a tight and harsh sound.

2   Remind singers of where resonance occurs in the body (refer to section on voice production and the physiology of singing in chapter 2). Each singer must learn to recognise when they are singing with resonance and how

to achieve this. Ask singers to hum with lips closed and the throat open, having practised raising and dropping the soft palate, and feel the sensation of buzzing in the lips and nose and sinus cavities.

3 Ask singers to start with an open-lipped 'hyng', which closes the soft palate, on each note, singing a descending scale, and feeling the resonance in the nose and sinus cavities. Then move into adding 'ah' on each note, opening the soft palate, and retaining the resonance, as in the example which follows. There should be a careful transition between the two sounds, with the mouth not overly open.

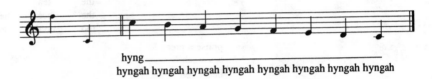

hyng _____
hyngah hyngah hyngah hyngah hyngah hyngah hyngah hyngah

4 To combine focus with resonance, and connect this with support, the following exercise is useful. It should be sung slowly, the ticks in the example represent the breaths being taken in. Be aware of the 'tummy tucks' necessary to control the breath and support the voice as the notes are sung.

mah    mah    mah    mah    mah    mah    mah    mah

5 Sustaining resonance and support through a phrase can be practised using the following exercise. It also helps singers to connect leaps. Use more open vowels on the top notes in these exercises, otherwise singers may have to modify the top vowel sounds (see later).

| see | fah | see | fah | see |
|-----|------|-----|-----|------|
| too | far | to | my | car |
| my | soul | has | gone | down |
| to | know | him | so | well |

## Trouble-shooting
### *Modifying vowels*

To sustain resonance and focus when the music demands more closed vowel sounds, such as 'ee' and 'oo' on top notes, singers may find it necessary to modify vowels in order not to tighten up. Repeat the above exercise with different vowels and suggested modifications, as in the following example. Modification should be done with care, not starting *too low*; for sopranos the vowels usually need attention at D♯ -E; for altos C-D; for tenors and bases follow the same pattern as for sopranos and altos.

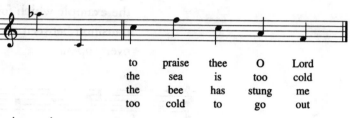

|      |        |      |       |      |
|------|--------|------|-------|------|
| to   | praise | thee | O     | Lord |
| the  | sea    | is   | too   | cold |
| the  | bee    | has  | stung | me   |
| too  | cold   | to   | go    | out  |

praise = prehs
sea = seh
bee = beh
cold = cald

### *Correcting shrillness*

Resonant sound is brilliant but not shrill. In aiming for a rounded sound, do not encourage singers to over-emphasise 'head voice', a fault commonly found in young choristers. To achieve the effect of each note 'glowing', the following exercises help singers to 'develop down', or use the totality of voice.

*Exercise 1*

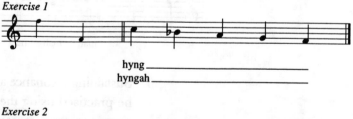

hyng _____
hyngah _____

*Exercise 2*

hyng _____
hyngah _____

*Exercise 3*

legato - no bumps in sound

hum _____

*Exercise 4*

hum _____ ah _____ m

*Exercise 5*

hum _____
humah _____

## Intonation and singing in tune

This is at times a problem for all choirs. Flat singing, which usually sounds too 'airy' or 'breathy', may be due to poor breath support and lack of appropriate vowel modification on high notes (see above). It can also result from overly loud singing. It may be an individual or ensemble problem. If the former, you may have picked it up in auditioning. It is also caused by fatigue and low energy levels, being too hot, poor morale, and the relative humidity or dryness of the environment. Loss of focus and resonance resulting in poor intonation can be improved by the exercises noted above, particularly the 'hyng – ah ' ones.

Sharp singing, usually the lesser of the two evils, often results from tightening up and over-blowing, produced by anxiety and insecurity. Knowing the notes well can improve this problem, as the singers can relax into the music. Your attitude can also induce a calming effect.

A 'witch-hunt' for the transgressors is not conducive to better intonation, even if you are aware of individuals with particular problems. A major factor in improving matters is the encouragement of your singers to listen to themselves and to each other. The following exercise is useful in problems of intonation.

one - two   one - three   one - four   one - five   one - six   one - seven   one - eight
ee   ah   ee   ah   ee   ah   ee   ah   ee   ah   ee   ah   ee   ah

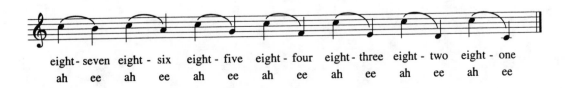

eight - seven   eight - six   eight - five   eight - four   eight - three   eight - two   eight - one
ah   ee   ah   ee   ah   ee   ah   ee   ah   ee   ah   ee   ah   ee

When the problem lies in keeping tunefulness in leaps, try the following exercise. Ask singers to aim for balance and equal temperament between each note. Do not rush the exercise.

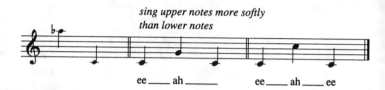

*sing upper notes more softly than lower notes*

ee ___ ah ___ ee ___ ah ___ ee

Keeping in tune in descending phrases, when the tendency is to flatten, can be improved by exercises which move in semi-tones up and down the scale.

Preventing the flattening of repeated notes can be achieved by helping singers to maintain breath support and focus.

## Pitching accurately

The foregoing 'trouble-shooting' section has referred so far specifically to problems of tunefulness related to resonance and focus. These are different from problems of pitching notes accurately when singing in parts. Exercises which enable singers to imagine themselves into the notes should encourage them to take risks without fear of retribution and, wherever possible, flow from the particular piece of music being rehearsed. The following exercise improves security in pitching notes as well as a greater sense of ensemble singing.

### *Exercise*

**Key changes**

Ask singers to sing the notes appropriate to their voice (ie soprano, alto, tenor, bass) changing appropriately as you tell them to change key. Play the first chord. Then either call out the name of the next chord, or show on a large piece of paper the notation, in notes or letters, of the next chord. When they are secure in singing the changed chord, repeat the process.

## Legato singing

Bel canto is the underlying inspiration for emphasis on 'legato' in choral singing.

*Exercises*

**Purpose**

To achieve a fluid and connected line.

**Time**

Up to 5 minutes at each rehearsal.

**Activities**

*Exercise 1*

ee - eh - ah,    ee - eh - ah,    ee - eh - ah,    ee - eh - ah,    ee - eh - ah.

see - red - car,    see - red - car,    see - red - car,    see - red - car,    see - red - car.

see - blue - car,    see - blue - car,    see - blue - car,    see - blue - car,    see - blue - car.

*Exercise 2*

ah ———————————————— yeh ——————————— ah

*This may be sung twice,*
*the second time doubling the speed.*

*Exercise 3*

ah ————————————————————————————————

*Exercise 4*

see     fah     see     fah     see

my     soul     has     gone     down

the     sun     has     gone     down

## Voice agility
*Exercises*

**Purpose**
To develop vocal flexibility and proper placing of sound. Be aware of maintaining a relaxed jaw in the higher range especially.

**Time**
As necessary.

**Activities**

*Exercise 1*

ah    eh    oh    ee,   ah    eh    oh    ee.
Al - le - lu - ia,   Al - le - lu - ia.
coo   coo   coo   coo,  coo   coo   coo   coo.

*Exercise 2*

ah    eh    oh    ee,   ah    eh    oh    ee.
Al - le - lu - ia,   Al - le - lu - ia.

*Exercise 3*

repeat

nim nim nim nim nim nim nim nim nim
tu   tu   tu   tu   tu   tu   tu   tu   tu
mee meh mah moh moo _____

*Exercise 4*

ee _____
eh _____
ah _____

*Exercise 5*

*very legato – think of a circle*
*in order to connect the leaps*

ee  ah  ee  ah  ee  ah  ee  ah  ee  ah  ee  ah  ee

*Exercise 6*

ah _____
ee _____

## Extending range and compass

This can be achieved over time as singers become less shy of very high or very low notes. The following exercise is helpful. Play the chord of F, asking the choir to sing the octave softly to 'oo' ascending and descending, the basses and altos singing an octave lower than the sopranos and tenors. Repeat this to 'ai' *mezzoforte* and to 'ee' *forte*. Repeat in the chord of F sharp, and rising by semitones until the chords of B or C.

Additionally, the following exercises, which encourage flexibility, can be used in higher ranges, the emphasis on lightening the voice as it ascends. It is also helpful, as the voice ascends, to hold hands at waist level and push them down into the floor as singers reach the higher notes. This stops the head tipping upwards and facilitates the sensation of looking down on the notes.

*Exercise 1*

ah

*Exercise 2*

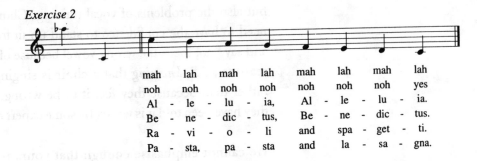

| mah | lah | mah | lah | mah | lah | mah | lah |
|-----|-----|-----|-----|-----|-----|-----|-----|
| noh | noh | noh | noh | noh | noh | noh | yes |
| Al - le - lu - ia, | | | | Al - le - lu - ia. | | | |
| Be - ne - dic - tus, | | | | Be - ne - dic - tus. | | | |
| Ra - vi - o - li | | | | and spa - get - ti. | | | |
| Pa - sta, pa - sta | | | | and la - sa - gna. | | | |

*Exercise 3*

Bel - la  si - gno - ra
La - sa - gna  ver - de

# Some Concluding Thoughts

Having either stayed with us throughout this brief discourse on 'giving voice', or dipped into certain aspects of it, we hope that you are heartened by the immense potential power you hold with regard to improving choral singing. We realise that many of you will have had no particular training in choral development. Many, as David Hill suggests are now, or started as, primarily organists, with the added responsibility of training a choir:

'The English church music scene produces its own dichotomy: an organist is wrongly assumed to be a choir trainer; conversely, choir trainers can end up as terrible organists. I'm not suggesting that we should split the posts of organist and choir master; rather, I believe that we should treat the areas entirely separately. Perhaps when we are training organists we should not only address the practical aspects of conducting, such as how to beat time and so on, but also the problems of vocal training. Church musicians need to have the confidence to stand up in front of a choir and say "no, that's the wrong vowel because of the following reasons . . .", *knowing* that a choir is singing incorrectly, rather than because they feel it to be wrong, and because they have been told it is wrong by some expert teacher.'[1]

We cannot emphasise enough that yours is a privileged position, though it may at times feel daunting. Henry Coward thought that it took five to ten years to become a good choir trainer and conductor and to achieve a really musical sound with a choir. This may be disheartening to those of you starting out. The vicissitudes of modern life may make it impossible for you remain with the same choir for this long. Don't despair! As we have repeatedly said, ours is not a counsel of perfection so much as a recognition of the need to go on learning and to being open to new ideas about how to improve choral singing.

We hope the ideas we have put forward will trigger your own forays into exploring approaches which are new to you and give you the confidence to build on your existing expertise in this, so often challenging, but infinitely rewarding activity of 'giving voice'.

# Notes

**CHAPTER 1**
**The Singers and the Singing**

1 For more information about the history of chorus, *The New Grove Dictionary of Music and Musicians* published by Macmillans, is an excellent source. We have referred specifically to the 1980 edition p 341 ff

**CHAPTER 2**
**The Voice**

1 *Caduceus Magazine,* issue 19
2 For more information refer to *The New Grove Dictionary* Vol 17, p 345 ff
3 Novello and Co. London, undated
4 Quotation from *The New Grove Dictionary* Vol 17 p 345
5 op cit
6 For much of the following description we are indebted to the *New Oxford Companion to Music*, O.U.P. 1983 Vol 2 p1939 ff
7 Refer to the *New Oxford Companion to Music,* op cit for more detail
8 ibid
9 op cit

**CHAPTER 3**
**The Psychology of Singing**

1 William McVicker Interview, *Musical Times* 1988
2 ibid

**CHAPTER 4**
**The Choir Director**

1 cf a series of articles entitled 'The Reluctant Choir-trainer', for the Royal School of Church Music, Trevor Ford, London
2 op cit
3 op cit
4 ibid

**CHAPTER 5**
**Conducting: Role and Techniques**

1 'A Choir Training Lecture' given to the Royal College of Organists, Oct 11 1989
2 op cit

**CHAPTER 6**
**The Rehearsal**

1 op cit
2 'The Reluctant Choir Trainer' series
3 op cit
4 op cit
5 op cit

**CHAPTER 9**
**Voice Production and Projection**

1 'William McVicker Interview', *Musical Times*
2 op cit

**SOME CONCLUDING THOUGHTS**

1 'William McVicker Interview', *Musical Times*

# Index

# Acknowledgements

The publishers wish to express their gratitude to the following for permission to reproduce copyright material:

Oxford University Press, Walton Street, Oxford OX2 6DP for extracts from *The New Oxford Companion to Music* ed Denis Arnold (1983).

The editor of *Church Music Quarterly*, the journal of the Royal School of Church Music for extracts from 'The Reluctant Choir Trainer' series.

Cherry Gilchrist for an extract from her article in *Caduceus Magazine*, issue 19.

Novello & Co. Ltd. 8/9 Frith Street, London W1V 5TZ for extracts from *Choral Technique and Interpretation* by Henry Coward.